Age-Proofing Your Memory...

...The Ultimate Brain Builder

AGE-PROOFING YOUR MEMORY...

...The Ultimate Brain Builder

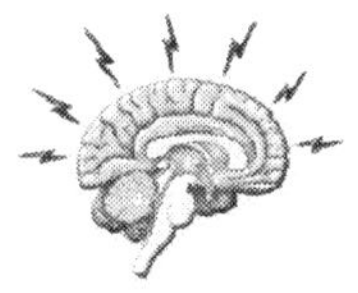

Arlene R. Taylor
Sharlet M. Briggs

Stimulate intelligent/creative memory with brain aerobic exercises

Thriving Brain™

Success Resources International
Napa, California

Arlene R. Taylor, PhD
Sharlet M. Briggs, PhD

Requests for information should be addressed to:

www.ThrivingBrain.com
sharlet@ThrivingBrain.com

www.arlenetaylor.org
thebrain@arlenetaylor.org

ISBN # 1-887307-99-0

Edited by: David H. Hegarty,
Barbara Bothe, Dolores J. Gardner, Len Moors,
Leona Running, PhD, and Margie Penkala

Cover design: David Eastman
www.EastmanCreations.com

Illustrations by Brent Fjarli used by permission.

Printed in the USA

Contents

Publisher's Note

Unfortunately, in this 21st Century it becomes necessary to remind readers that each person is responsible for his/her own choices, actions, and behaviors. The authors have made all reasonable efforts to ensure that the information in this book is accurate and up-to-date. However, there are no representations or warranties provided regarding the information—expressed or implied.

The information and resources offered are for general educational and informational purposes only and do not present an in-depth treatment of specific research findings or topics. They are not intended to take the place of professional counseling, medical or psychological care, or recommendations from healthcare professionals.

Be sure to consult with your physician or healthcare professional before you make lifestyle changes or add physical exercising to your daily regimen.

The publisher, authors, and editors expressly disclaim all responsibility and any liability (direct or indirect) for adverse effects from the use or misuse of concepts presented herein.

If you find errors/typos in this book, please know that they are there for a purpose. The authors wanted to write something for everyone, and some people enjoy looking for mistakes.

Dedication

This book is dedicated to the many individuals whose brains have stimulated, inspired, and affirmed ours—and who are role-modeling dynamic and gracious aging. May their tribe increase!

Preface to the Ultimate Version

Three additional versions are available:

- *Age-Proofing Your Memory... Using Scripture.* This book is a variation on *Age-Proofing Your Memory...the Ultimate Brain Builder* in that some of the brain aerobic exercises are based upon Biblical names and terminology. References to denominational dogma and specific theological perspectives are avoided.

- *Age-Proofing Your Memory... Using Scripture—Mormon Version.* Some of the brain aerobic exercises are based on Biblical (King James Version) names and terminology and *The Book of Mormon.*

- *Age-Proofing Your Memory... Using Scripture—Catholic Version.* Some of the brain aerobic exercises are based upon scriptural references from *The Holy Bible, Revised Standard Version, Second Catholic Edition* (with ecclesiastical approval of the United States Conference of Catholic Bishops), 1966 Edition; revised according to the *LITURIAM AUTHENTICAM,* 2002.

Two new books are available:

- *Age-Proofing Your Brain—21 Key Factors You Can Control*
- *Age-Proofing Your Immune System*

Preface

Wet Your Whistle…

The human mind, once stretched by a new idea, never regains its original dimensions.
—Oliver Wendell Holmes

Your brain is unique. Yes, the brains of human beings are more alike than they are different regardless of gender, race, ethnicity, and almost anything else you can name. And yet each is unique in terms of structure, function, and perception.

Since each brain's developmental pattern is unique, no two brains are alike. Even the brains of identical twins differ in structure, function, and perception.

Human brains have the same general features and if you could look at them with the naked eye would appear quite similar. However, the specific configuration of bumps and fissures along the outer layer or cortical surface is unique to your brain.

Throughout your lifetime, circuit connections between neurons are made stronger or weaker according to the way in which you use them. Not only that, your brain tends to become more unique with age.

Estimates are that the brain contains about the same number of neurons in each brain system. The way in which your neurons are connect, however, and the richness of your dendritic branches, is a distinct reflection of your genetic endowment and your life experiences.

How much do you know about the brain? Unfortunately, many people know very little about brain function in general and their brain in particular. Fortunately, current brain-function information from a variety of brain-imaging modalities is more available than ever before and can help you *meet your brain in a new way.*

A Fast Pass through the Brain

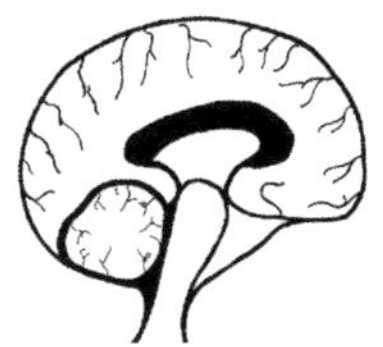

Human Brain Cutaway

The drawing to your right looks very much like your brain might appear if you cut it in half through the nose toward the back of the head. Some sections would be visible to the naked eye even without the aid of a microscope.

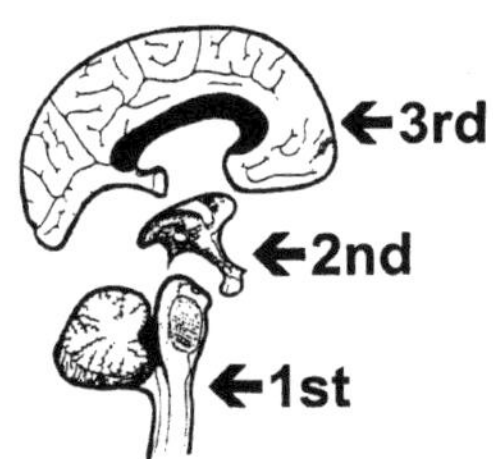

This drawing pulls portions of the cutaway apart. In order to keep information more user-friendly, the triune or three-layer model is used in this book. It shows the frontal lobes along with their pre-frontal portions (behind the forehead) as one layer. Some researchers count the prefrontal lobes as a fourth layer.

First Brain Layer

The first brain layer includes the brain stem and the cerebellum. It houses subconscious thought, automatic reactions to stressors (e.g., fight-flight, tend-befriend, and conserve-withdraw) takes in sensory data, and runs muscle programs involved in repetitive activities. It also helps to regulate heart rate and breathing.

Second Brain Layer

The second brain layer, also houses subconscious thought. It is known as the pain-pleasure center or limbic system. It contains several little brain organs including the amygdalae and hippocampi that are believed involved with storage of memory and recall functions.

Metaphorically, the hippocampi can be compared to an internet search engine. Not surprisingly, these tiny twin organs are important to memory functions. When you want to recall information, your *search engine* goes to work collecting all the requisite associations and reassembling them into what you want to recall.

Third Brain Layer

The third brain layer has a plethora of names including gray matter, cortex and neo-cortex, cerebrum, and thinking brain. This portion of the brain houses conscious thought and what are often referred to as executive functions, including planning, decision-making, goal setting, problem-solving, willpower, conscience, judgment, moderating behavior, and morality. Not surprisingly, the frontal lobes are important to memory functions.

Third Layer – Four Chunks – Eight Lobes

This drawing shows the third brain layer from yet another perspective. A natural fissure divides it into two hemispheres, each of which is further divided into two portions:

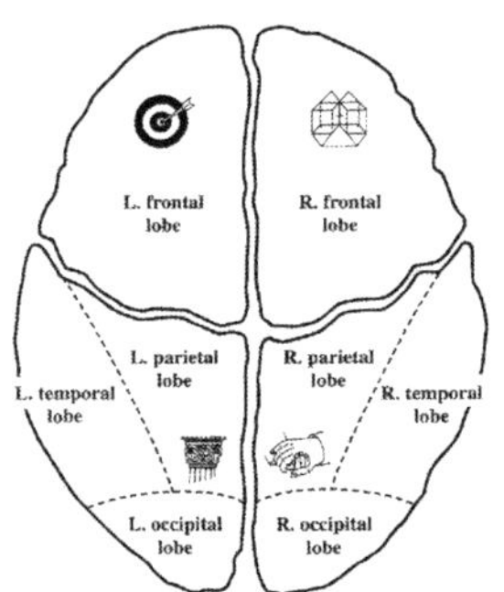

- Two frontal divisions that contain one lobe each – the right frontal lobe and the left frontal lobe

- Two posterior divisions that contain three lobes each:

  - Occipital lobes have to do with functions such as visuospatial processing, color discrimination, and motion perception

  - Temporal lobes are highly associated with memory functions (e.g., may actually contain some discrete memory banks) and sound processing

  - Parietal lobes contain a variety of motor functions, perception of muscle position, the integration of sensory information from various parts of the body, and so on

Reading in Your Brain

The above information can help you to better understand what happens when you read and how that process involves complex functions throughout your brain.

The drawing below of the third brain layer is a variation of the one on the previous page. Here different symbols have been included.

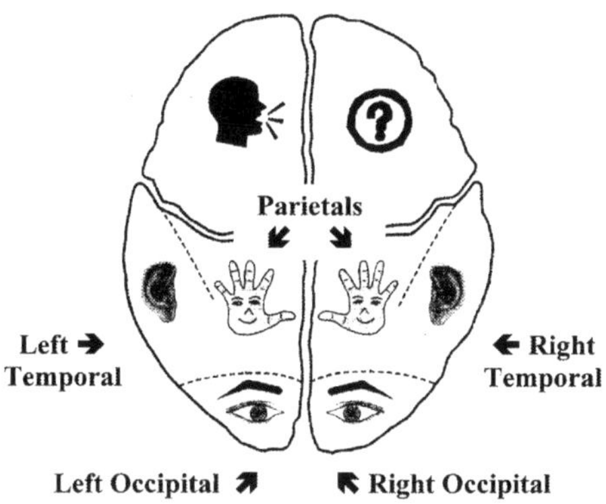

When you read, as you are doing now, electrical impulses representing the words travel through your visual system to the occipital (visual) lobes, where letter-recognition occurs.

Next, areas in the parietal and temporal lobes merge the letters and recognize that those letters form words. In whichever language you can read, your brain will recognize the letters and words.

In the left temporal lobe and in Broca's area (left frontal lobe where audible speech occurs), a sound is associated with the word. Even when you read silently, the areas of your brain associated with processing sound are as active as they would be if someone were reading the story aloud.

In Wernicke's area of the left temporal lobe, a meaning is associated with the word. Finally, functions in the parietal lobes synthesize both the sound and the meaning of the word, turning the words into ideas.

You may also create internal representational pictures in the right frontal lobe. Since every brain is different, including its experiences and education, the pictures your brain creates will be unique to your brain.

Describing Your Thoughts to Others

You may try to convey in words the pictures you create in your brain or mind's eye. When those to whom you are speaking respond, "I see what you mean," or "I get it," or "I understand," they do—at some level.

Unless they could actually see inside your head, however, their brains do not perceive what your brain does in exactly the same way. That's one excellent reason for giving up all expectations of another brain ever completely understanding yours and vice versa.

This would be a good place to mention that not only does no one really understand his/her own brain but also no brain is capable of mind-reading another's.

The Faces of Memory

Memory can be defined as the mental faculty that gives you the ability to think of past experiences or learned information. Memory is not a single cognitive process and all are not stored in a single area of the brain (except perhaps for some memory banks in each temporal lobe).

Memories are believed to be stored as *associations* (small bits of related information) throughout portions of your brain. This involves processes such as retention, recall, and recognition. It results from chemical changes among neurons in several different areas of the brain. Of course, memory has many different *faces.*

Immediate, Short-, and Long-Term Memory

Data may be retained in the brain for varying amounts of time, assuming the brain has taken in the data.

- Immediate memory lasts for just a few seconds. You see something from the side window of the car as you are speeding down the road. Later on you may recall very little or few details of what you actually saw.

- Short-term memory lasts for only a few minutes. For example, long enough for you to read a phone number and then dial it.

- Short-term memory may be transferred into long-term memory, which may last for an entire lifetime or for as long as the neurons are alive.

No one recalls absolutely everything. Generally the brain retains what it is interested in or what it perceives is necessary for safety and survival. The loss of memory due to disease or injury is referred to as amnesia.

Neurons and Glials

Two general categories of brain cells have been identified: neurons—thinking cells, and glials—supporting cells. Memory is possible because of your neurons. The glial cells occur in the brain in a ratio of nine or more to one neuron.

Imagine what your life would be like if you had nine people whose only purpose and goal was to feed, support, and take care of you 24/7. Such a deal!

Neurons are electrically excitable cells in the nervous system that process and transmit information. There may be 100 billion neurons in the adult human brain, give or take a few billion.

Compare this to the estimated number of neurons in the brain of a fruit fly, a mouse, or a monkey.

- Fruit fly: 100,000
- Mouse: 5 million
- Monkey: 10 billion
- Human: 100 billion

In reality, 100 billion neurons are somewhat of an uncomprehendable number. If you were to stack one hundred billion pieces of paper, the stack would be about 5000 miles high—the distance from San Francisco to London. Yet 100 billion neurons give or take a few billion, are crammed inside your bony skull.

Initially the directions for crafting your brain were contained in your genes, contributed to you from the sperm and egg that came from your biological donors (whether or not you were raised by them).

Recent estimates are that you have about 25,000 genes that are ranged along your 46 chromosomes. That number is totally dwarfed by the thought of 100 billion (100,000,000,000) neurons with perhaps more connections between them (1,000,000,000,000,000) than there are atoms in this universe.

Neurons never actually touch each other. They reach toward each other across a gap (synapse) with their axons and dendrites (tiny hair-like filaments that project out from the neuron).

Axons can be as long as the person is tall, which means that neurons are the longest cells in your body. Axons are usually covered with a thin coating of myelin that increases the speed at which messages can be sent. Think of axons as the door out of the neuron. Axons take information away from the cell so it can be transferred to another cell.

Dendrites, on the other hand, are always short—less than a millimeter in length. They are covered with little dendritic spines or hairs. Think of dendrites as doors into the neuron. They collect information and bring it into the cell. Some brains have difficulty *learning* because there are too few dendrites on its neurons or too few dendritic spines on each dendrite. Therefore, it is difficult to pull information into the cells.

Education Pays

When your brain learns new and challenging information, this process grows dendrites and dendritic spines. This enriches your brain. This is one reason your parents and teachers may have encouraged you to get an education. No wonder! Studies have shown this is one way to age-proof your brain. In fact, you may want to enroll in a course that interest you—now!

Studies in several different countries have reported that the risk of Alzheimer's disease may be reduced by challenging the brain through formal study or its equivalent.

Education pays!

Growing Dendrites

The following drawing portrays two neurons. Notice the difference in numbers of dendrites between the challenged and unchallenged neurons.

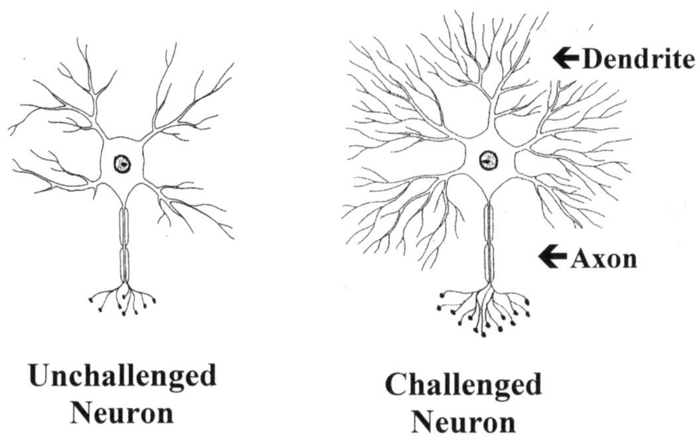

Any intellectually-challenging activity is believed to stimulate dendritic growth, which adds to the neural connections in the brain. It also is believed to help the axons and dendrites stretch out to their full length. This minimizes the synaptic gap between neurons and helps to make thinking (the transfer of information between neurons) happen more quickly and easily.

Care of Your Brain

One of the best things you can do for your memory is to take very good care of your brain. Not surprisingly, one way to take care of your brain is to ensure that a sufficient amount of oxygen gets into your blood stream.

Oxygen comes into your lungs through the air you breathe and is then transferred to red blood cells that transport the oxygen to cells in your brain.

Growing up, you may have been taught that the best way to breathe was to stand up straight, stick out your chest, and hold in your abdomen. It turns out this is not an optimal position for deep breathing.

Abdominal breathing is the ticket!

In fact, some believe you can increase the amount of oxygen that reaches your brain through *brain breathing* and they advocate doing this on a daily basis.

The formula for brain breathing is:

- Breathe in through your nose to a count of four
- Hold your breath while counting to twelve
- Exhale through pursed lips to a count of eight

Take a dozen brain breaths every day. Endeavor to do this in pure fresh air. Avoid polluted environments such as those that contain secondhand smoke, vehicle exhaust, or high levels of particulate matter in the air.

With that thumbnail sketch, it's time to dig into practical applications that can help you age-proof your memory.

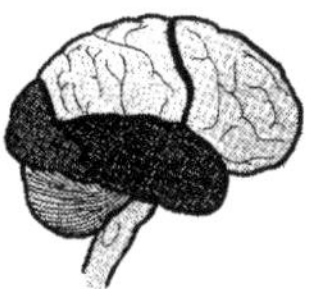

Think of the exercises and information presented as "fun education" that can help you retard the onset of symptoms of aging, slow down memory loss—and strengthen intelligent/creative memory.

Brain Tip

Hang out with smart people and be proactive in challenging your memory on a daily basis

Brain Bits

Here are several strategies for challenging your memory—you're on your own for finding smart people with whom to hang out:

- Play games that make new connections between ideas (e.g., a brick can be used as a hand-weight)
- Read aloud for ten minutes every day
- Listen to audio books on a regular basis; minimize TV viewing
- Do simple math calculations as quickly as you are able, always trying to increase your speed
- Solve all types of puzzles
- Hone your sense of humor and look for the humor in everyday living
- Rehearse what you want to remember, using both visualizing and auditory processing

Chapter 1

Introduction

Your Memory Matters…

For the unlearned old age is winter;
for the learned it is the season of the harvest.
—Talmud

"I don't remember." "I can't recall." "I'm afraid I'll lose my memory."

Sound familiar? Somehow aging and memory loss have become synonymous in the minds of some. Those who experience gerontophobia, the fear of aging, can become so anxious they may even forget exactly what they are anxious about!

Three of the most important challenges many people face with the aging process are:

- Physical health
- Balance and coordination
- Cognitive decline

Of the three, cognitive decline—losing your memory, more specifically—is the biggest concern for some.

Benign Senescence is the terminology used for a type of age-related forgetfulness. While this phenomenon is commonly observed, it is by no means universal. You may be able to retard its development, if not completely prevent it.

Yes, some people's overall brain mass may start shrinking in their 60's and 70's. That's the bad news. But for many people, taking positive action to keep the brain challenged may moderate this.

It is important to balance that information with good news. Brain researchers believe that:

- The human brain is just as capable of "learning" in the second half of life as in the first half

- In people who are physically healthy, the brain's learning capability does not likely change a great deal as they age

- While it may take a bit longer to learn something in later life, the chances of recalling it are likely also as good as when you were younger

Because of these encouraging findings, this book concentrates on the positive. It focuses on the activities and life-style aspects that may make a difference in your life and in the lives of those who are dear to you.

People who tend to move through the aging process successfully share specific characteristics and activities that appear to help prevent memory decline and alterations in cognition.

This book outlines some of those characteristics and activities that have been revealed through research studies. Thanks in part to new sophisticated brain-imaging technology, scientists can now offer educated suggestions for strategies to help keep your memory sharp. Such a deal!

21st Century Information

Fortunately you live in a period of earth's history when research is burgeoning. Scientists are coming to understand that lifestyle choices may play an even bigger role than people realize, particularly in terms of memory. Contributory factors range from daily brain aerobic exercises to dietary choices. Studies are beginning to validate the full impact of what can be achieved through challenging brain stimulation.

Some of those studies are from a relatively recent genre known as brain function. This new science was made possible by the advent of brain-imaging equipment, although it does include research from several broad fields, including anatomy, physiology, biology, chemistry, neurology, psychology, and psychiatry, to name just a few.

Personalize This

What does this mean to YOU? It means that YOU can help retard the onset of symptoms of your own aging. In some cases, if you've already "lost it," you may perhaps even restore some of the lost functionality.

You may be able to strengthen specific types of memory and improve your recall ability. Since each brain is different, decline symptoms and improvements will be unique to each brain.

The goal is to develop a lifestyle that protects your brain insofar as it is possible to do so, and that allows you to retain all your functions in as high a state of functioning for as long as possible.

Types of Memory

Several different types of memory have been identified. All are useful in life for storing and recalling different types of information. Two of them tend to decline with age, while one can actually improve with age.

Explicit or Declarative Memory

This type of memory involves the ability to recall information consciously and be able to state it to someone else. It refers to remembering facts, functions that involve the hippocampus and conscious-thought portions of the brain. It is the most likely to be damaged with brain injury.

Explicit memory can be divided into two categories:

- Semantic - factual information (e.g., name, age, address, phone number, counting, license number). Semantic memory is believed within the capacity of many animals.

- Episodic - autobiographical memory (e.g., specific personal experiences including emotions that were present during the event or experience). Episodic memory is thought to be characteristic of humans.

Explicit memory tends to decline with age. It can be beneficial to hone recall of information. Repeat poems, songs, and trivia from memory. Share stories from the past with your family and friends.

Implicit or Nondeclarative Memory

This type of memory involves behavioral, emotional, and perceptual information that is reflected in behaviors and actions without conscious thought. It involves recalling how to do things. Implicit memory can also be divided into two categories:

- Somatosensory (bodily) – the organization of memory on an iconic level (relating to pictures and images rather than words) such as bodily sensations, behavioral enactments, nightmares, and flashbacks.

  This also involves actions such as tying shoes and swimming. Because the brain controls all your movements, it tends to remember them in a form of body memory. Body memories, like learning to ride a bike, tend to stay in the brain as long as the neurons are alive.

- Cellular memory – epigenetic nonverbal information-energy stored at a cellular level. It is not genetic in the sense that it utilizes genes and chromosomes, but is likely formed by strands of protein in the cell nucleus.

Implicit memory also tends to decline with age. Again, some benefit can be derived from honing this type of memory, especially in terms of continuing to practice physical skills.

Intelligent Memory

The third type of memory is intelligent or creative memory. It involves the ability to work with concepts and ideas. While there are limits to what the brain can memorize by rote repetition, there appears to be unlimited capacity for learning concepts and processing ideas.

Intelligent/creative memory is composed of three elements:

- Your memory pieces (e.g., information, knowledge, experience)

- The connections and associations your brain has made among them

- The distinctive mental processing that occurs through mixing and matching pieces and connections. This can provide insight, help with problem-solving, enhance your creativity, and so on.

Intelligent/creative memory can strengthen with age.

That is good news. Great news, actually!

While you can benefit from almost any type of mental stimulation, consensus among some brain-function specialists is that you should devote the majority of your time, energy, and efforts on the type of memory that can strengthen with age.

Brain Aerobic Exercises

The puzzles and activities in this book are designed to help stimulate your neurons and strengthen intelligent/creative memory. Solving the puzzles and completing the activities may help you learn to think more effectively, brainstorm *outside the box*, develop higher levels of creativity, hone your imagination, and perceive information in a new way. This can contribute to age-proofing your memory.

In the preparation of this book, the authors tapped into a plethora of current brain-function research. Each chapter contains both puzzles and brain-function information including Brain Tips and Brain Bits. Taken together they are designed to exercise your brain in different ways and to provide proactive brain-function information. When practically applied, they can help your brain and body move through the aging process more gracefully.

Your brain may find some puzzles easier than others or even like some better than others. To get the maximum benefit, try to solve all of them.

Brain Benders

Brain Benders are one type of brain aerobic exercises included in this book. If you have not written or solved Brain Benders before, following is an example to get you started.

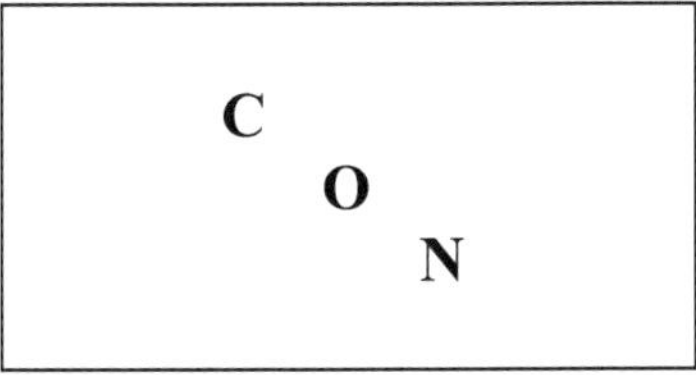

The three letters form "con." Notice that the letters are not in a straight line but move downward. As you study this puzzle your brain may come up with ideas such as:

- This *con* (short for convict) is going down
- Or *con* is short for a scam
- Or condescending based on the letter arrangement
- Or something else your brain might think of…

In some of the brain-benders puzzles it can be important to note the relative position of the words to each other or to the box itself. It can also help to read the puzzle words aloud so your brain "hears" the sounds. There are no "right" or "wrong" answers—just what each brain figures out.

Hundreds more of these puzzles are available in Arlene Taylor's book entitled *Brain Benders.*

Daffynitions

Daffynitions are another type of brain aerobic exercises. The word itself is a generic term indicating a pun format (a humorous play on words). It involves the reinterpretation of an existing word on the basis that it sounds like another word or words.

Your brain likely knows the common definitions of the words in question. Read the words aloud and listen to the way they sound. Select the unusual definition that best matches the sound of the word.

Take the word Daniel for example. The letters *iel* sound something like yell. An unusual definition could be:

Yelling or calling for Dan.

Matching the unusual definitions to the words can help to create new and multiple associations in your brain.

Sequential Series

The Sequential Series require your brain to analyze a sequence of letters, numbers, or figures and select one of the available options to complete the series. Take some time with these. Instruct your brain to analyze and evaluate each series for possible constructs that could provide clues to the best option.

Word Puzzles

Some puzzles ask you to fill in the blank. Try to do this first by tapping into your rote memory. Others ask you to find the hidden words or unscramble words. Still others provide clues to answer the question "Who am I?"

Write the answers by holding a pen/pencil in your nondominant hand. This will provide additional exercise to the opposite side of your brain.

Perception Puzzles

Brain Perception puzzles offer your brain the option of viewing things in more than one way. These puzzles often involve a spatial form of thinking outside the box and can help to strengthen intelligent/creative memory.

Simple Arithmetic

Studies have shown that you get more bang for your buck when you exercise your brain with simple rather than complex arithmetic problems.

Each chapter has addition, subtraction, multiplication, or division tables. Continually try to beat your own time for arriving at the answers. Create your own arithmetic questions and continue practicing.

Mazes

A maze is a puzzle in the form of a complex branching passage. You need to use your wits to find a route through the maze. For some there may be a solution provided while for others you can figure it out on your own.

Sudoku

This logic-based puzzle became popular in Japan about 1986. It is now well-known in many parts of the world. The objective of the Sudoku-like puzzles in this book is to fill a 9×9 grid so that each column, each row, and each of the nine 3×3 boxes (also called blocks or regions) contains the required numbers, letters, or symbols used only *one* time each.

Left, Right, and Whole Brain

Brain aerobic exercises can strengthen functions in the left hemisphere, functions in the right hemisphere, and functions / coordination between the hemispheres.

Left-brained puzzles are designed to strengthen functions related to word recall, word recognition, reading, and writing. (For most brains these functions are located in the left hemisphere although they are reversed in some brains.) These include:

- Crossword puzzles
- Scrambled words puzzles
- Find the word puzzles
- Fill in the blank
- Simple arithmetic
- Which word, letter, or number doesn't match

Right-brained puzzles are designed to strengthen functions related to recognition of objects or symbols, spatial-visual concepts, and visual perception. (For most brains these functions are located in the right hemisphere although they are reversed in some brains.) These include:

- Select the matching objects
- Find the object that doesn't match
- Count the number of squares
- Mazes

Whole brain puzzles and activities are designed to strengthen functions in both hemispheres and/or coordination between hemispheres. These include:

- Write using your nondominant hand
- Brain Benders
- Daffynitions and other riddle-type questions
- Brain perception puzzles
- Sudoku-type puzzles

Flexibility

One goal of brain aerobic puzzles is to help you hone mental flexibility—to maximize divergent outside-the-box thinking while minimizing convergent inside-the-box thinking. Inside-the-box thinking is when you review the available information and are expected to arrive at only one conclusion.

Honing mental flexibility gives you practice in viewing things from an opposite angle. Remember, in a huge storm the trees that are flexible are the ones most likely to survive.

You may recall reading that Dr. Edward Jenner solved the smallpox puzzle by studying people who did *not* get the disease. Previous researchers had focused on who *did* get smallpox. That's a great example of out-of-the-box thinking!

Do what you can to take good care of your brain. You're the only one who can, and you'll only have yourself to thank as you age!

Work Your Brain

To get the most benefit to your brain, brainstorm your own solutions before you peek at suggestions in the Solutions section (aka Revelations).

A desirable goal is to obtain a minimum of 30 minutes of challenging mental exercise each day. Include brain aerobic exercises designed to strengthen intelligent/creative memory.

Whenever possible, read aloud and stimulate both cerebral hemispheres as you go through this book. Listening to stories being read aloud can also help to stimulate intelligent/creative memory.

Check out www.ThrivingBrain.com for a collection of stories on CD especially designed to stimulate your sensory systems.

It Matters

Stimulating your brain matters. Studies have shown that stimulating the brain with brain aerobic exercises may slow down the aging process, stimulate neurons and dendritic development, and strengthen intelligent/creative memory—at least at some level.

If you already are on this journey, use this book as an adjunct. If you aren't, start now! According to Gray Small, MD, author of *The Memory Bible,* it's never too late to begin:

> *As soon as you start to change your lifestyle for the better, you'll begin to repair yesterday's damage.*

Get busy and have fun during the aging process. It's going to happen anyway, so you might as well take control of as much of it as you can and laugh as you learn.

You'll be glad you did—and so will everyone who knows you!

You're on your way!

Brain Tip

Read aloud for at least ten minutes a day

Brain Bits

Brain-imaging studies have shown that more of your brain is stimulated when you read aloud than when you read silently. Increased activity occurred in a component of Broca's area located in the left hemisphere, and stimulation to the right hemisphere occurred in a way that was different from what happened during silent reading.

In *The Read-Aloud Handbook*, Jim Trelease reported on studies related to reading aloud and learning. Reading aloud to a child is the single most important factor in raising a reader. It can improve their reading, writing, speaking, listening ability, vocabulary, and attitudes about reading. Some believe it can help the adult brain in a similar way.

Reading aloud or listening to others read aloud can give your brain additional stimulation—because sounds are involved. For a list of original stories on CD designed to stimulate intelligent/creative memory, refer to: www.ThrivingBrain.com/products.

Whenever possible, read aloud and stimulate both cerebral hemispheres as you go through this book.

Chapter 2

Time's Awasting...

Memory is the library of the mind.
—Francis Fauvel-Gourand

Several different forms of memory have been identified. All are useful in life for storing and recalling different types of information. Two of them tend to decline with age, while one can actually improve with age.

Explicit or declarative memory is the ability to recall information consciously and declare it to someone else (e.g., your name, address, and phone number). This type of memory tends to decline with age.

Implicit or nondeclarative memory involves behavioral, emotional, and perceptual information (e.g., tying shoes, riding a bicycle, swimming, bodily sensations) that is reflected in behaviors and actions without conscious thought. Implicit memory also tends to decline with age.

Intelligent or creative memory involves an ability to learn concepts and process ideas as opposed to rote memorization. It provides insight, enhances creativity, and helps with problem-solving. The good news is that intelligent/creative memory can strengthen with age.

Because of this, it is prudent to spend most of your time and energy honing skills related to this type of memory.

Intelligent/creative memory is composed of three elements:

- Memory pieces stored in your brain (e.g., facts, figures, information, knowledge, experience)
- All the connections and associations you have made among those memory pieces
- The distinctive mental process of mixing and matching pieces, connections, and associations

The Eyes Have It

Focus on the short line for a few moments.
What does your brain perceive?

Double Header

Insert the missing numbers in each series (formulas differ for each set).

Set #1

1, 2, 3, 7, 8, 9, 19, 20, 21 43, 44, 45, 91, 92, 93,

___, ___, ___, 379, 380, 381, ___, ___, ___

Set #2

1, 2, 4, 7, 11, ___, 22, 29, ___, 46, 56,

67, ___, 92, 106, 126, ___, 184, 202, 21,

241, ___, 284

Nothing like Flying

What does your brain perceive?

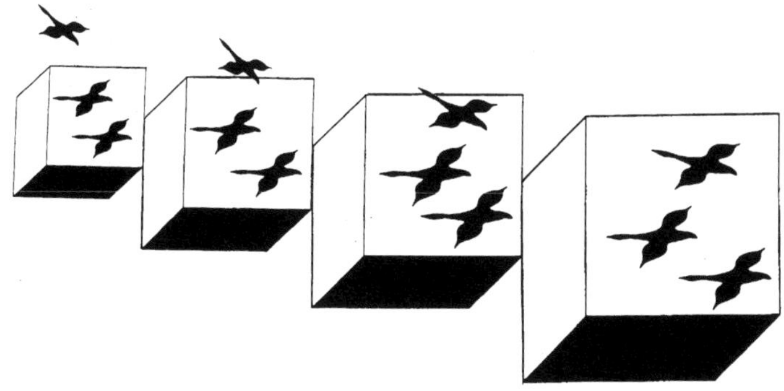

Start to Finish

Fill in the blank(s) to finish each series.

1. 4 8; 12 16; ___, ___
2. O T T F F S S E, ___
3. 2 4; 6 18, ___. ___
4. S M T W T F ___
5. 6 9; 12 6; 18 9; ___, ___
6. J F M A M J ___
7. 2 10; 3 18; 4 28; ___ ___
8. N M J L T ___
9. T T T F F S S ___
10. F S T F F S ___
11. O T T F F S S E ___
12. Z X C V B N ___
13. 4 5 8 17 44 ___
14. 13 57 911 1315 1719 ___
15. D N O S A ___

Flocking Together

What does your brain perceive first?
Does the position of the figure or it composition make a difference?

Yee-Haw

What does your brain perceive?

Did You Know?

Many have wondered if time travel is theoretically and practically possible.

According to Jeremy Irons, we all have our time machines. Some take us back, they're called memories. Some take us forward, they're called dreams.

Money Matters

Complete the puzzle so that the required numbers and symbols are used only once in every 3-by-3 box, every row, and every column: # % $! ? & 7 8 9

	%		7		8			!
				?		$		8
				&		?	7	
	!						8	#
			?		%			
$	&						%	
	9	%		8				
8		&		7				
!			&		#		9	

Did You Know?

Exposure to perceived high psychological stress for prolonged periods of time may accelerate one's biological age by as many as 17 years.

Would You Believe it?

Answer the questions.

1. Do the words flammable and inflammable have the same or opposite meaning?

   - ❑ Same
   - ❑ Opposite

2. What is a philatelist?

   - ❑ Boxer
   - ❑ Writer
   - ❑ Stamp collector

3. The sky is blue because?

   - ❑ Of the Law of Nature
   - ❑ Of earth's atmosphere
   - ❑ Of the North and South Pole
   - ❑ It reflects off the blue ocean

4. Where does "G'day mate" mean hello?

   - ❑ S. America
   - ❑ E. Africa
   - ❑ Australia
   - ❑ Ireland

5. Who was the second US President?

   - ❑ Samuel Adams
   - ❑ George Washington
   - ❑ John Adams
   - ❑ Abe Lincoln

Odd Signs

Complete the puzzle so that the required numbers and symbols are used only once in every 3-by-3 box, every row, and every column: 1 ○ 3 □ 5 △ 7 ◇ 9

	1	○	5					
◇	5							□
				3		◇		9
			□	△		5	3	
			9		7			
	△	□		5	◇			
5		9		1				
□							△	3
					3	7	9	

True or False – Half and Half

Charismatic movements (so-called) are *affective* and tend to be aligned with the right hemisphere of the brain. This in contrast to more traditional movements that are more likely to be aligned with the left hemisphere of the brain.

Stars Get in Your Eyes

Count the differences

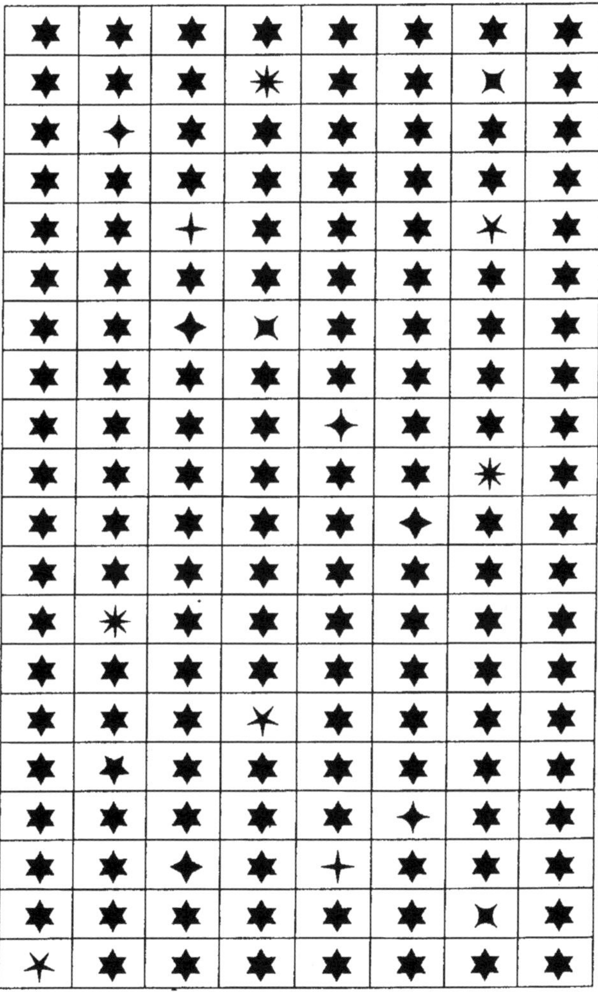

Brain Benders 2-1

<table>
<tr><td>1.

PAR
T
O
N</td><td>2.

HA IR
H AIR
HAI R
HA IR</td></tr>
<tr><td>3.

E A
H D</td><td>4.

E
V
O
M</td></tr>
<tr><td>5.

IS IS IS IS IS
SI SI SI SI SI</td><td>6.

C C C C C</td></tr>
<tr><td>7.

HE AC
AD HE</td><td>8.

TIS
IT</td></tr>
<tr><td>9.

EAITR</td><td>10.

REHTONA 1</td></tr>
</table>

Negotiations Heading South

What does your brain perceive first?
What stories can it imagine?

Balancing Act

What does your brain perceive?

©Brent Fjarli

Brain Tip

Develop personal life satisfaction based on what is important to you and your brain

Brain Bits

A study conducted by Bernice Neugarten at the University of Chicago found that the most important factor in healthy aging is *life satisfaction.* In the study, older adults who exhibited the following attitudes and perspectives tended to have better health:

- Enjoyment of daily activities
- Optimism
- A positive and worthwhile self-image
- Feeling one's life has meaning
- Satisfactory achievement of major goals

A 23-year study by Yale University involving more than 600 people aged 50 and over showed that individuals with positive thoughts about aging lived an average of 7.5 years longer than those with negative thoughts about old age.

Behavior is organized around beliefs. What you choose to believe creates your own personal reality. Develop an attitude that life circumstances are manageable and meaningful, that you are in control of your life to some degree, and that your life has meaning.

Chapter Three

Use It or Lose It...

Each receptor molecule remembers how many times it has been stimulated and whether it was over or under stimulated.
—Candace Pert

The human brain is the exciting new frontier of the 21st Century. Much as early navigators traveled and mapped the world, pioneer explorers in the field of brain function and brain imaging are shedding light on the most amazing organ in your body!

How many times have you heard the phrase *use it or lose it*? So often that it has become a cliché? Studies have shown this is as real for the brain as it is for muscle tissue. Although not muscles, neurons function in much the same way; they tend to strengthen with exercise and shrivel with disuse.

The more your neurons are challenged, the stronger they become and the farther they stretch their projections (axons and dendrites). This shortens the space between neurons (synapses) and makes it easier for them to exchange information.

Challenging mental exercise on a daily basis may help to delay the onset of symptoms of aging!

Brain Benders 3-1

1.	2.
Brain	**GEGS** **EASY**
3.	**4.**
SOMEWHERE **WOBNIAR**	**ONCE** **EMIT**
5.	**6.**
GNIKOOL	**ARREST** **RU**
7.	**8.**
T O O L **O O** **O O** **L O O T**	**S M** **W M I N** **I G**
9.	**10.**
BATHEATLE	**H I J K L M N O**

Change in the Weather

Count the differences

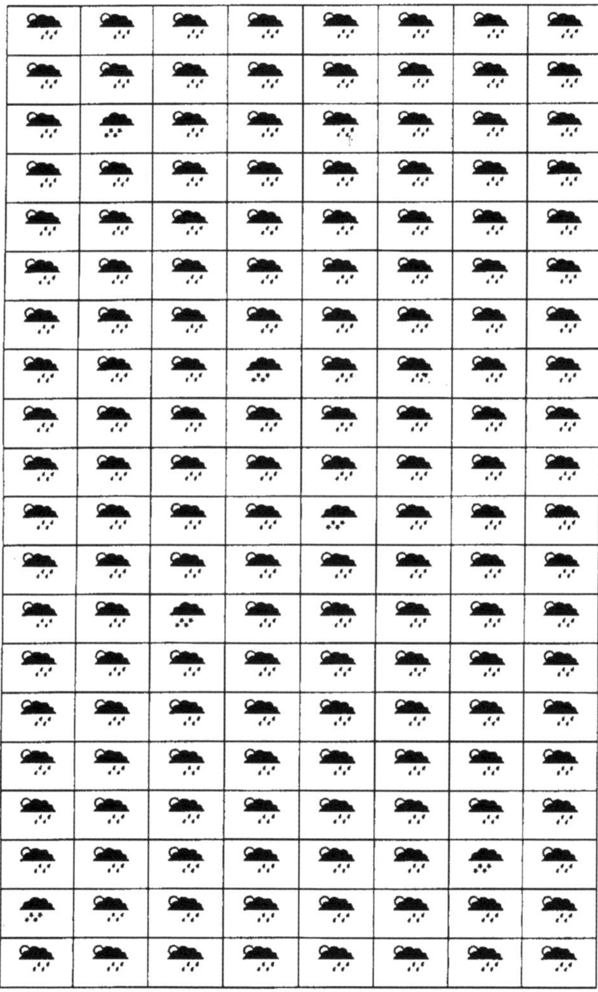

Brain Benders 3-2

<table>
<tr><td>1.</td><td>2.</td></tr>
<tr><td>G G E
G E G
E G G</td><td>O   O
U I U
T N T</td></tr>
<tr><td>3.</td><td>4.</td></tr>
<tr><td>LEFT
HCNUL</td><td>JOANB</td></tr>
<tr><td>5.</td><td>6.</td></tr>
<tr><td>S'TAHW</td><td>DEEF</td></tr>
<tr><td>7.</td><td>8.</td></tr>
<tr><td>RITE
GNORW</td><td>K   R
CLOCK
C   O</td></tr>
<tr><td>9.</td><td>10.</td></tr>
<tr><td>| D |
| A |
| E |
| R |</td><td>TS
II
MD   MY
EE</td></tr>
</table>

Two Times Two

Complete the puzzle so that the required letters are used only once in every 3-by-3 box, every row, and every column: FOUR MINDS

I		F			S	U		R
			M	I	N	D		
M	S	D				I	N	O
	F				I		D	
O				M				N
	U		S				O	
D	R	O				M	I	F
			I	R	O	N		
N		S			M	O		U

True or False – Vividly

The brain can quite easily tell the difference between what you actually experience and what you vividly imagine in your mind's eye.

Famous Lines

Solve for the phrase by William Shakespeare

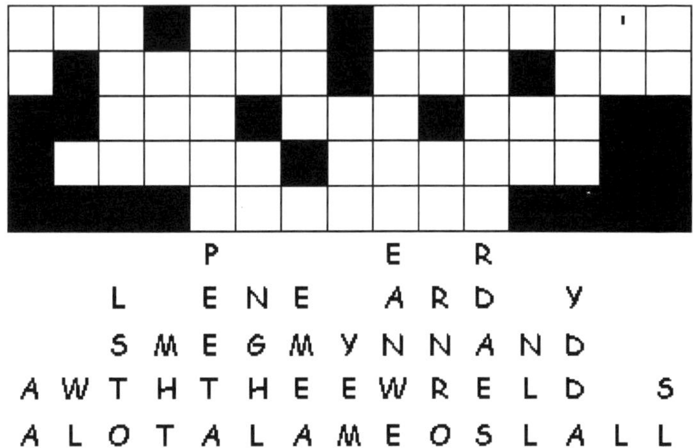

The Winner Is

What does your brain perceive?

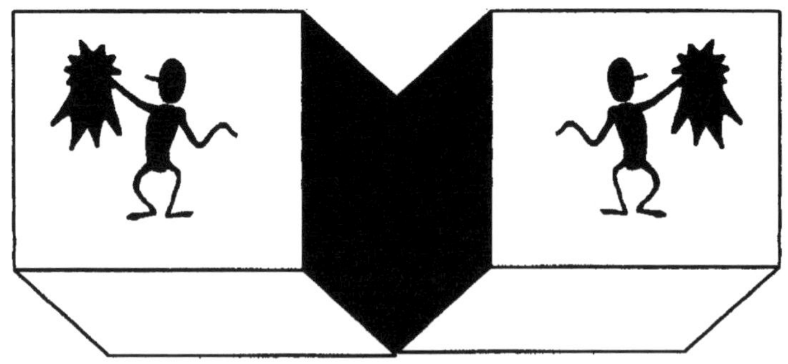

Did You Know?

According to Richard Restak in his book entitled *Mysteries of the Mind,* the human brain is the most intricately organized and densely populated expanse of biological real estate in the world.

One cubic millimeter of brain tissue—roughly the size of a grain of coarse sand—contains approximately 100,000 neurons that can make about ten billion connections or synapses. These neuronal connections, places where the brain cells meet, are more important than the brain's total number of cells.

At the rate of 1 connection per second, some have estimated it would take 32 million years to count the synapses (connections) in the average brain.

In Your Cups

Create a story about what your brain perceives.

A Fine Kettle of Fish

Solve the following riddles.

1. It's strange. If you use me dry, the wetter I become. What am I?

2. You used a knife to cut my head, yet you weep above me when I'm dead. What am I?

3. As my anniversary approaches I collect diamonds. On the first day of the month I collect one diamond, on the second day I collect two, and so on. So by my anniversary I will have collected 276 diamonds altogether. On which day of the month is my anniversary?

4. In the song *The Twelve Days of Christmas,* how many gifts did I receive altogether?

5. While I am alive, I do not grumble and make no noise when you walk on me. When I am dead however, I grumble quite loudly. What am I?

6. Jill likes carrots but not tomatoes, turnips but not lettuce, and peanuts but not pecans. Following the same logic, will she like radishes or cucumbers?

7. I cannot see anything although I may have many eyes! What am I?

Hearts are Bustin' out all over

How many hearts and how many differences does your brain perceive?

Between You and Me

What do these suggest to your brain?

True or False – Really?

In general, devote minimal effort to challenging yourself in areas that are energy-exhausting for your brain.

Rather, play to your strengths, especially in your work life. Concentrate your efforts in areas of talent (innate giftedness) and maximize time spent in areas that are energy-efficient for your brain.

Take Care of Your Heart

What does your brain perceive?

True or False – Ages

Although your chronological age cannot be altered, both your psychological and biological ages can be speeded up or slowed down. Naturally, slowing them down is the preferred choice!

Flower Fantasia

How many flowers and how many differences does your brain perceive?

*	*	*	*	*	*	*	*
*	*	*	*	*	*	*	*
*	*	*	*	*	*	*	*
*	*	*	*	*	*	*	*
*	*	*	*	*	*	*	*
*	*	*	*	*	*	*	*
*	*	*	*	*	*	*	*
*	*	*	*	*	*	*	*
*	*	*	*	*	*	*	*
*	*	*	*	*	*	*	*
*	*	*	*	*	*	*	*
*	*	*	*	*	*	*	*
*	*	*	*	*	*	*	*
*	*	*	*	*	*	*	*
*	*	*	*	*	*	*	*
*	*	*	*	*	*	*	*
*	*	*	*	*	*	*	*
*	*	*	*	*	*	*	*
*	*	*	*	*	*	*	*
*	*	*	*	*	*	*	*

Brain Tip

Increase your personal knowledge about the aging process and take conscious steps to retard the onset of aging symptoms

Brain Bits

Interestingly enough, the process of aging is somewhat flexible, perhaps more so than has been believed in the past.

In an article entitled *Mind Games,* Tom Geoghegan wrote that there is now good scientific evidence to show that exercising the brain can slow, delay, and protect against age-related decline.

According to Depak Chopra, MD, because the mind influences every cell in the body, human aging is fluid and changeable. It can speed up, slow down, stop for a time, and even reverse itself.

The average person has strong enough longevity genes to live to age 85 and maybe longer. Some research suggests that, biologically, humans potentially can live from 100-120 years.

Awareness is the first step on the ladder of positive change. The more knowledge you possess about the aging process, the better. The next step is putting into practice what you have learned!

Chapter Four

Lend Me an Ear...

The human brain is the most important musical instrument of all.
—Keith Lockhart

Music engages regions of the brain involved with paying attention, making predictions, and updating an event in memory. You perceive music in more than one way, too.

Unimpaired, your brain hears the musical sounds through your ears, plus your skin senses the music as the sound waves beat against it.

Of all the arts, music has the closest link to the brain and body. Its rhythms are analogous to breathing, walking, and heartbeat. It has enormous power to communicate emotion, an ability that appears to reflect a built-in process beyond cultural conditioning.

As George Szell put it, "In music one must think with the heart and feel with the brain."

Music can shift attitudes as well as feelings. It can hurry you along or put you to sleep, tell you stories, prompt you to dance, influence the type of products you purchase, promote healing, sharpen your creative powers, and cause shivers of pleasure.

Music can alter the brain's electrical rhythms. And your heart rate will synchronize with music, speeding up or slowing down accordingly. In short, music is powerful!

More than 300 years ago the French composer François Couperin declared children should begin studying instruments by age six or seven. Learning music at an early age can lead to long-term gains in activities that require the use of reasoning skills, of which math and science are two prime examples.

Studies have shown that the corpus callosum (one of the bridges connecting the right and left brain hemispheres) is 10-15% thicker in musicians who started training before the age of 7 than in nonmusicians. Musical training can impact both how the brain works and how it is built (e.g., can enhance learning, memory, and intelligence).

Did You Know?

When you sight-read music, especially at the piano, you recruit and rapidly coordinate almost every major area of your brain. There are few other activities that challenge so many portions of your brain at the same time.

Musical Metronome

Complete the puzzle so that the required numbers, letters, and symbols are used only once in every 3-by-3 box, every row, and every column: COUNT 1 2 🕒 4

		U			1	T		
	1			🕒			4	
N			U			1		
	T	4	N	O				
🕒	C							2
				1	🕒	4	O	
		1			T			4
	U			2			T	
		2	🕒			U		

True or False – Slowing

In music, slow tempos and minor keys tend to slow the brain's cortical and limbic areas.

Pairs Playing

Music can help bridge generations even as it stimulates the brain. The story is told of a musical encounter between Pinchas Zukerman, the brilliant violinist and conductor of Canada's National Arts Centre Orchestra, and his father, also a violinist.

The older Zukerman had an impaired right hand due to a stroke and had ceased playing his beloved violin.

One day while visiting his father in Israel, Pinchas held up a violin and asked whether his father would like to play a favorite concerto. Puzzled, the father reminded his son, "I don't have the right hand."

Smiling, Pinchas placed the violin in his father's undamaged left hand and, standing behind him, plied the bow as the two men played in harmony.

Two generations, two brains, and one violin. One man using his right hemisphere and left hand, the other his left hemisphere and right hand.

Did You Know?

Playing a musical instrument is one way to challenge the brain and give it a good workout. Playing a musical instrument exercises coordination between eye and hand and stimulates both the creative and logical portions of the brain.

Brain Benders 4-1

1.	2.
RATION__	**MOEKATVIE**
3.	**4.**
BRIDGE N E **O R** **W E** **H H** **E W** **R O** **E N**	**D C** **R O** **I A** **V S** **E T**
5.	**6.**
GNINNUR **FUMES**	**PENC** **IL**
7.	**8.**
DEAD	**TRADINSIDERING**
9.	**10.**
GET **DRAOB**	**YRD**

Did You Know?

The California Marsh Wren may sing as many as 120 themes in a given jam session. And humpback whales, capable of vocalizing over a range of at least seven octaves, have been found to use rhythms similar to those found in human music. They can sing in tune, and their songs contain refrains that rhyme.

Music Recall

Songs can help to coordinate hemispheric functions: the right hemisphere learns the melody while the left hemisphere learns the words. Think of a favorite song with words.

- Hum and then whistle the melody
- Recall the title and the words
- Identify the songwriter and singer

Now listen to a selection of music without words.

- Recall its title and identify the composer
- Recall the name of the performer(s)
- Pay attention to the music's "mood"
- Tap your hand to keep time to the beat

The Notes Have It!

Count the differences

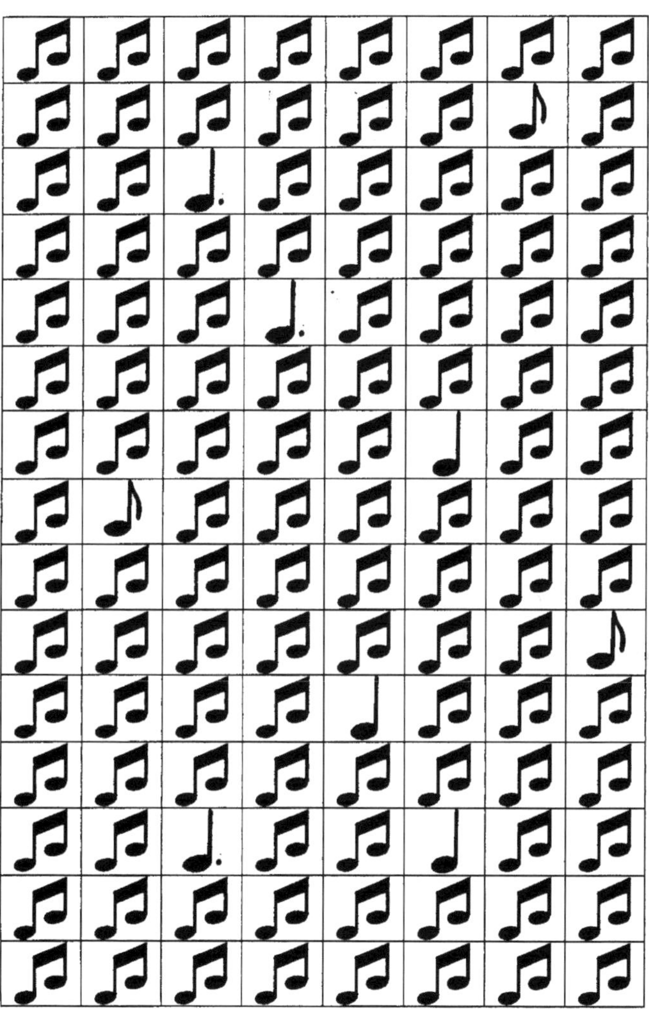

Brain Benders 4-2

1.	2.
BDOOGOOD **TRUEB UR**	**BATS**
3.	**4.**
✓ **ROUTINE**	**CLEAN**
5.	**6.**
ARRIVE **EMIT**	**BOWLING** **NEERG**
7.	**8.**
TANIAPIL	**KICK**
9.	**10.**
DECADE	**FLKCALABSH**

Musical Challenge

Complete the puzzle so that the required numbers and symbols are used only once in every3-by-3 box, every row, and every column: **1 ⏲ 2 🔔 3 ♫ 4 ♈ 5**

<table>
<tr><td></td><td>⏲</td><td></td><td>🔔</td><td></td><td>2</td><td></td><td>3</td><td></td></tr>
<tr><td></td><td></td><td>1</td><td></td><td></td><td></td><td></td><td>5</td><td></td></tr>
<tr><td>2</td><td></td><td>3</td><td></td><td></td><td></td><td>⏲</td><td></td><td>🔔</td></tr>
<tr><td></td><td></td><td>♫</td><td>⏲</td><td></td><td>3</td><td>🔔</td><td></td><td></td></tr>
<tr><td></td><td>2</td><td></td><td></td><td></td><td></td><td></td><td>1</td><td></td></tr>
<tr><td></td><td></td><td>⏲</td><td>4</td><td></td><td>♈</td><td>5</td><td></td><td></td></tr>
<tr><td>1</td><td></td><td>2</td><td></td><td></td><td></td><td>4</td><td></td><td>5</td></tr>
<tr><td></td><td>5</td><td></td><td></td><td></td><td></td><td></td><td>♫</td><td>3</td></tr>
<tr><td></td><td>4</td><td></td><td>5</td><td></td><td>🔔</td><td></td><td>⏲</td><td></td></tr>
</table>

True or False – Tandem

Songs can help to coordinate functions between the two brain hemispheres. The right hemisphere learns the melody while the left hemisphere learns the words.

Brain Benders 4-3

1.	2.
ARREST RU	PAHSALFN
3.	**4.**
NENIAPCK	BELSTABFREY
5.	**6.**
SDUPOLC	BATTAB P U
7.	**8.**
IT (inside a box)	EHSHERSELF
9.	**10.**
GROWInG	PITYTIP PITYTIP SAKE

Do You Hear What I Hear?

Count the differences

Brain Tip

Do yourself and the world a favor and become now the person you want to be when you are older

Brain Bits

It has been said that being young is beautiful, but being old is comfortable. Part of that comfort may come from learning to understand yourself better.

With time and increased awareness, you are better able to know what to give up in order to obtain what you need, and conversely, when to throw in the towel because the cost is too high. You figure out who you are innately and don't necessarily take the descriptions others have given of you at face value.

The aging process gives you that opportunity.

Your individual characteristics magnify with age and you actually become less like others and more like yourself. Become the person now you want to be then!

Identify the behavior you need to change and visualize yourself exhibiting that new behavior. This gives your brain a map to follow as it molds to the new ideal.

Chapter Five

As Smart as a Steel Trap...

Our memories can set us up for the potential of a better tomorrow.
—Sharlet Briggs

In order to achieve anything, you must first decide it is possible—that you are capable of it. That includes brain aerobic exercises! When your brain has done anything once, it is more likely to be able to repeat it with a slightly increased level of competence.

Watching television and videos tends to encourage mental passivity. The brain passively pictures what another brain has created.

Listening to stories being read aloud can do the opposite, as the brain actively creates pictures in the mind's eye. Solving brain aerobic exercises also challenges and stimulates your brains.

Intelligent/creative imagination is called into play during problem solving. Creativity begins in the brain and *every brain is creative.*

Keep in mind that activities usually identified as creative are often very narrowly defined according to specific cultural mores.

Half Moon Rising

Count the differences

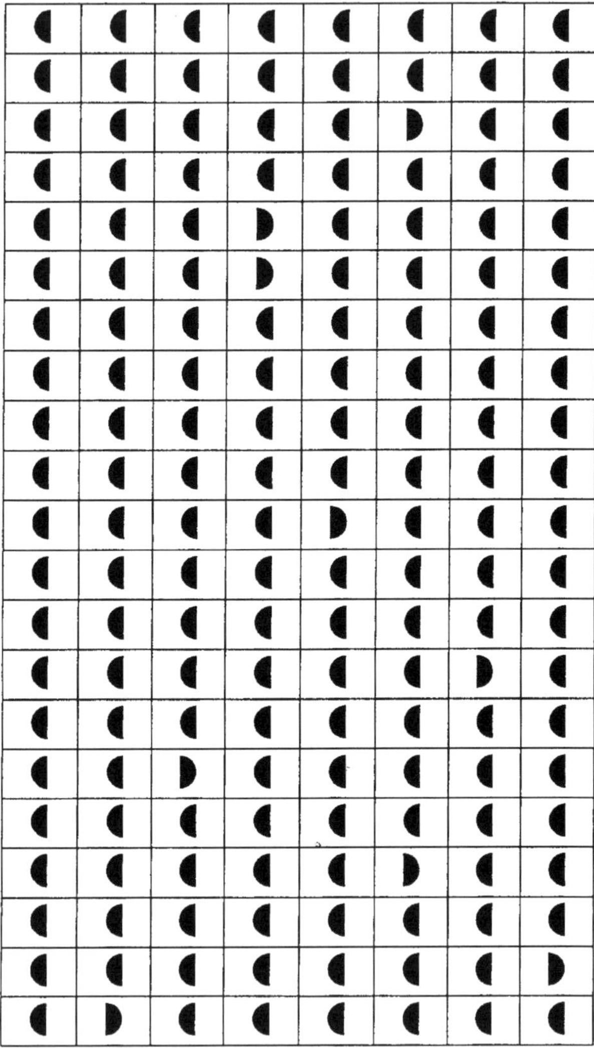

In the Blink of an Eye

Person 1: hold dollar-size paper at top edge and then release it

Person 2: place one hand level with bottom of paper and try to catch it

Now reverse roles.
When you see the paper released, the message travels from your eyes to your brain to be analyzed. Then the brain sends a message to your hand and fingers instructing them to catch the paper. By the time that happens, most people usually miss catching the paper, although it can depend somewhat on how the paper is dropped. Is your reaction time faster if you can predict when the other person will drop the paper?

Right Left, Left Right

Which way do the words face?

Square Off

Count the squares _______

Toot Your Own Horn

You probably already use a few tricks to boost your memory. If you don't know the answers to these questions, pay attention to mnemonic hints in *Solutions – Last Resort* found at the end of the book.

- Name the months that have 30 days
- Name the colors in a rainbow

The Same and Different

What do these have in common?

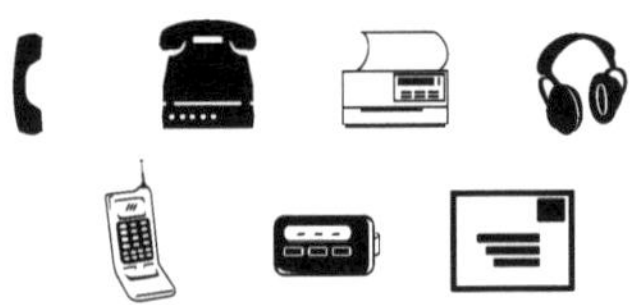

Square Has It

Count the squares ________

Name the Five American Great Lakes

- ____
- ____
- ____
- ____
- ____

List Possible Uses for an Orange

- ____________________ ____________________
- ____________________ ____________________
- ____________________ ____________________
- ____________________ ____________________
- ____________________ ____________________

Did You Know?

Compared with children's brains, adult brains tend to recall the meaning of an event and its emotional flavor rather than precise facts. As Diane Sawyer of Good Morning America put it, "Memory diffuses fact."

Squared Again

Count the squares ________

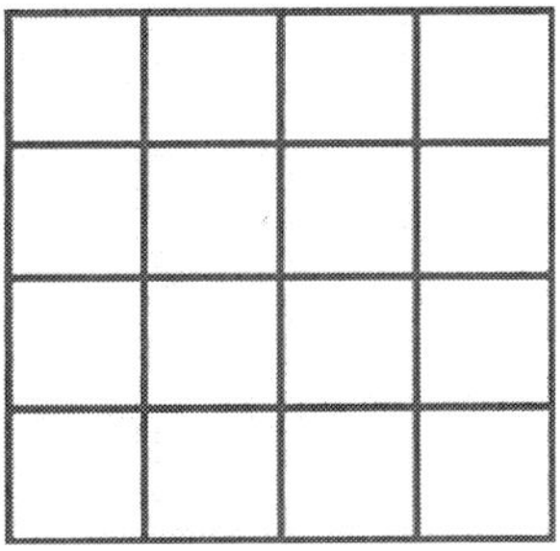

True or False – Einstein

Albert Einstein reportedly developed some of his best creative ideas when engaged in other activities such as walking, conversing, or daydreaming (e.g., imagining what it might feel like to ride on a beam of light and look back at a clock).

Square Wares

Count the squares ________

Did You Know?

While amnesiacs have no conscious recollection of any new experience, they can still learn many things non-consciously.

For example, when given suggestions during surgery that they will recover quickly, they subsequently spend less time in the hospital than patients not given the suggestions, despite having no conscious memory of what was said while they were under anesthesia.

Times Square

Count the squares _______

Peaks, Peaks, and More Peaks

1. Name the tallest mountain in the world.
2. Name the highest mountain in the world
3. Name the mountain range in S. Dakota and Wyoming
4. Name the mountain range that goes from California to British Columbia
5. Name the peak in Alaska that has an Native American name and an English name
6. Name the Japanese mountain that is sacred to the national Shinto religion
7. Name the mountain in Europe that is replicated in an American Theme park

Brain Benders 5-1

1.	2.
ESUOH	**K K K K** **K K K K K**

3.	4.
D **U O** **P W** **N**	**D** **N** **A** **T** **MISS**

5.	6.
ATTENTION	**worries**

7.	8.
M I N D	**GNITAE** **RUN**

9.	10.
WEDNESDAY	**FLOW**

Each of the 50 United States and District of Columbia has a Capital City

Can you name them?

Alabama
Alaska
Arizona
Arkansas
California
Colorado
Connecticut
Delaware
District of Columbia
Florida
Georgia
Hawaii
Idaho
Illinois
Indiana
Iowa
Kansas
Kentucky
Louisiana
Maine
Maryland
Massachusetts
Michigan
Minnesota
Mississippi
Missouri
Montana
Nebraska
Nevada
New Hampshire
New Jersey
New Mexico
New York
North Carolina
North Dakota
Ohio
Oklahoma
Oregon
Pennsylvania
Rhode Island
South Carolina
South Dakota
Tennessee
Texas
Utah
Vermont
Virginia
Washington
West Virginia
Wisconsin
Wyoming

The Location Is…Oops!

Where is the plaster bust?

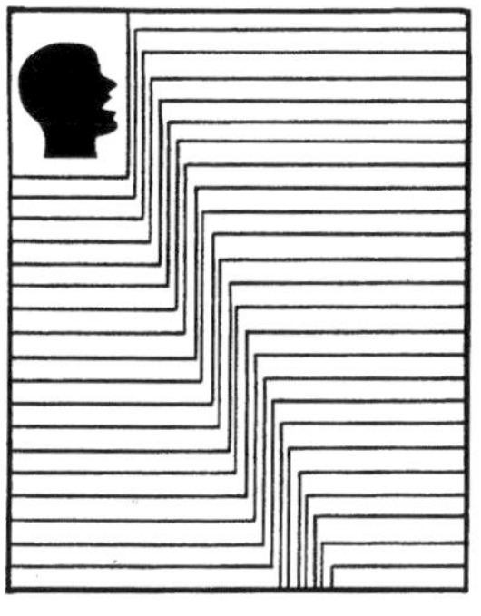

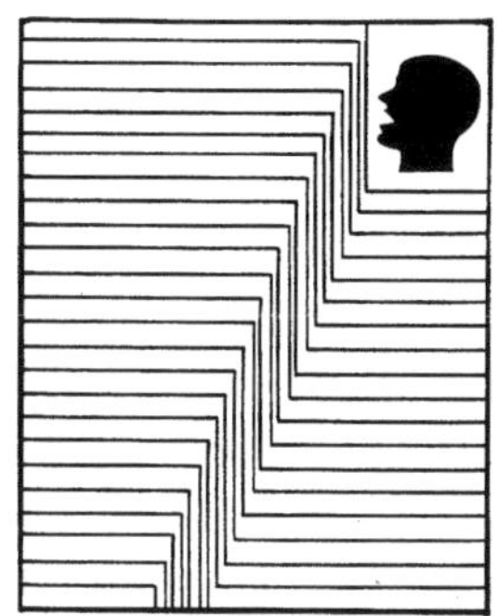

True or False – Neuroscience

Nutritional Neuroscience is a new medical specialty that studies how nutrients, vitamins, supplements, and other lifestyle factors can be utilized to increase brain power and prevent or reverse brain deterioration related to aging.

Brain Tip

Live a high-level wellness lifestyle and take personal responsibility for factors within your partial or complete control

Brain Bits

According to Robert Willix Jr., MD, author of the book *You Can Feel Good All the Time,* to a large degree you have at least some control over how healthy you are and how long you are going to live. That is great news!

Estimates are that between 40% and 50% of all the known factors that impact the aging process are within your partial or complete control.

Some of the factors that are typically within your control include your approach to:

- Good nutrition
- Sleep
- Physical exercise
- Mental exercise
- Deep breathing
- Spirituality
- Friends
- Relatives
- Daily water intake
- Relaxation
- Work
- A Higher Power
- Personal life vision
- Helping others
- Personal play time
- Stress management

Chapter Six

A Sense in Time Saves Mine…

To me, old age is always
15 years older than I am.
—Bernard M. Baruch

The three main sensory systems are:

- Visual – what you see with your eyes
- Auditory – what you hear with your ears
- Kinesthetic – what you smell, taste, touch, and sense (e.g., temperature, muscle position, the feel of clothing against your skin)

Human beings relate to each other and the world through the senses. Unimpaired, the brain can utilize all the senses. Most brains, however, are believed to possess a sensory preference. This refers to the type of sensory data that registers most quickly and intensely in their brain.

People tend to feel accepted and loved most quickly when they receive affirmation in their sensory preference. They also tend to gravitate toward environments in which their preference is acknowledged, provided for, and rewarded.

To identify your own sensory preference, download Taylor's Sensory Preference Assessment: www.ThrivingBrain.com/sensory

Stars, Stars, and More Stars

Rearrange the letters to identify the names of well-known individuals.

1. proah ywinref ____________________
2. archlie sonbig ____________________
3. binor tersbor ____________________
4. lleen sergeende ____________________
5. yarrl gink ____________________
6. ohjn maincc ____________________
7. racbar Abmao ____________________
8. Liyharl Tlnncoi ____________________
9. eppo nebedtic ixv ____________________
10. endrever libly ahmgar ____________________
11. geaninla ijlo ____________________
12. risronah dorf ____________________
13. aichmel helpps ____________________

When It Strikes, It Strikes

What does your brain perceive?

Divide

72 ÷ 8 =	12 ÷ 6 =	4 ÷ 4 =
27 ÷ 3 =	15 ÷ 3 =	60 ÷ 6 =
28 ÷ 7 =	10 ÷ 10 =	60 ÷ 10 =
49 ÷ 7 =	3 ÷ 3 =	32 ÷ 8 =
9 ÷ 1 =	6 ÷ 3 =	25 ÷ 5 =
20 ÷ 5 =	21 ÷ 3 =	2 ÷ 2 =
8 ÷ 4 =	4 ÷ 1 =	12 ÷ 4 =
27 ÷ 9 =	50 ÷ 5 =	33 ÷ 11 =
6 ÷ 2 =	64 ÷ 8 =	30 ÷ 5 =

Completion Times: ______,

______, ______, ______, ______

Did You Know?

Unless people sabotage the body's natural processes, several lines of evidence indicate that the human body is programmed to last until age 110 or so.

Match the Sport – Recall

1. Dallas Drake?
2. Babe Ruth?
3. Tiger Woods?
4. Magic Johnson?
5. Joe Montana?
6. Kristi Yamaguchi?

Food Is Good – Recall

Think of your favorite food.

- Picture it in your mind's eye.
- Is the taste sugar, salt, sweet, or sour?
- What makes it your favorite?

True or False – Sleep

The brain appears to need sleep more than the body. Sleep deprivation actually damages brain cells.

Brain Benders 6-1

1.	2.
WATER (boxed) **SALMON**	**LINE**
3.	**4.**
OERIDINGDOR	**MESMERIZED REH**
5.	**6.**
PAPERERAPAPER	**PLAGNINNURCE**
7.	**8.**
COLLABURT	**KOOLYOU**
9.	**10.**
GNIPMUJ **JUMPING**	**<u>50</u>** **50 50 50** **50 50**

School Days – Recall

Think about your school days. Did you attend public or private schools? Were you home-schooled? Did you take correspondence courses? What is your favorite school-days memory?

Did you have some favorite teachers? What is it about them that stuck in your mind? Tell someone everything you can recall about your first school experience.

Holiday Trivia – Recall

Think of your family's favorite holiday.

How did they celebrate?
Which holiday is your personal favorite? Identify the reasons that make it your favorite. Is it because of the time of year, the food, where you go to celebrate, or because of the other people involved?

Acting – Recall

Did you ever participate in a school play or community pageant? If so, what was the name of the play and what was your part? Did any family members attend your performance? What is your strongest memory about your performance? Describe the performance to a friend.

I Beg Your Pardon!

Count the differences

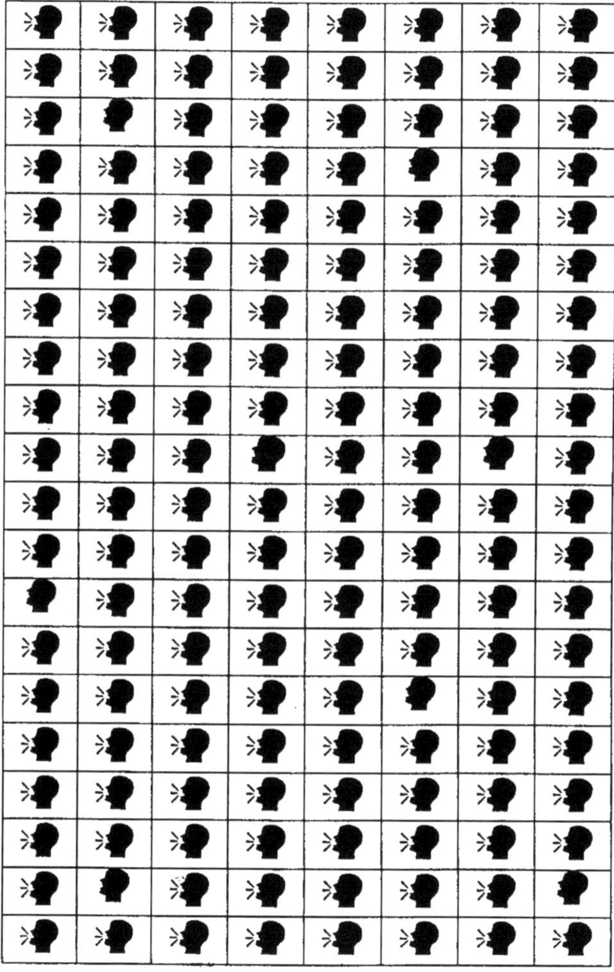

Strike While the Iron Is Hot

Fill in the blanks. Reading them aloud may help to trigger your auditory recall.

1. There are 1000 ________ in a __________
2. There are thirty ________ in one _________
3. There are 1760 ________ in one ___________
4. 39.37 _________ equals one ___________
5. Six city ________ equals one ____________
6. There are twelve _______ in one ________
7. There are three _______ in a _______
8. There are 5280 ________ in a _________
9. One bushel equals ______ quarts dry measure
10. One gross equals a ________
11. One peck equals ______ quarts
12. 128 fluid ________ to a US _____________
13. One inch equals _____ centimeters
14. One kilogram equals 2.2 ___________
15. One ___________ equals 1.6 miles
16. Four ___________ equal one gallon
17. One bushel equals 32 quarts or 8 ___________
18. One acre contains ________ square rods
19. The pi (π) ratio for any _______ is _______

Brain Benders 6-2

1.	2.
ALLdlrow	**MEDIA S**

3.	4.
C O M P Y N A	**HOTOH HANDLELDNAH**

5.	6.
VERSE + VERSE =	**TROUBLE**

7.	8.
RECOV __ __ __	**6 + 5 = 12**

9.	10.
D N A T MISS	**YTPM UD YT PM UH**

True or False – Heredity

For most people, actual heredity has far less impact on longevity and health than lifestyle choices and personal behaviors.

Stairs and Towers

What does your brain perceive with these figures?

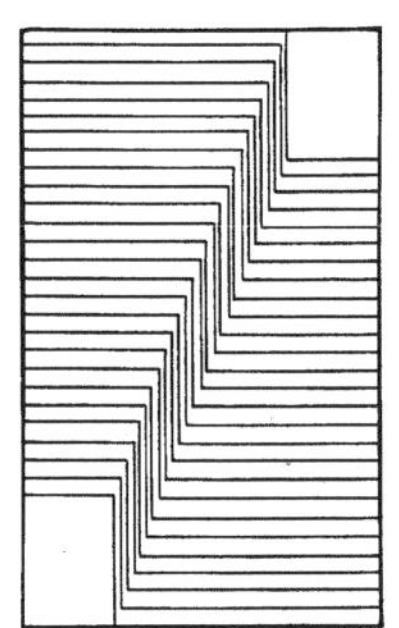

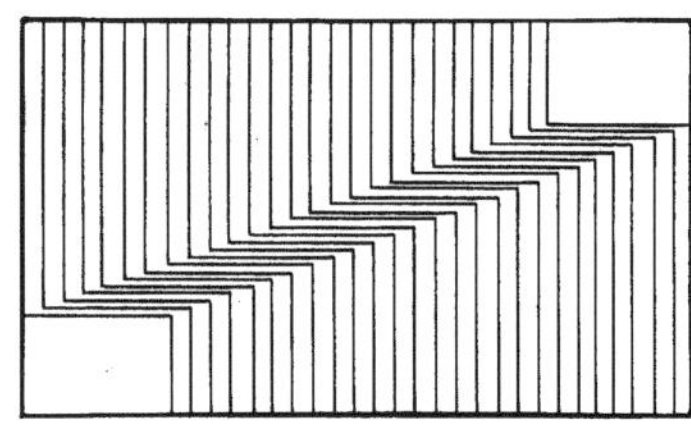

Did You Know?

Jigsaw puzzles challenge the brain as it makes visual judgments about where pieces belong, mentally rotates the puzzle pieces, directs your hands as they manipulate pieces, and shifts attention from small to big-picture pieces and back again.

Finding the correct pieces can stimulate the production of dopamine, a chemical that can help to improve learning and memory.

Brain Benders 6-3

1.	2.
DELUFECAEPATH	**DRIVDEEPSLIMIT**

3.	4.
GNIKROW **DEADLINE**	**LATE** **ETAL** **NOC**

5.	6.
NEOP **DINNERENNID** **DINNERENNID**	**DEIRROW** **NOTHING**

7.	8.
A A **H L L H** **W E W**	**H I D** **I** **N** **G**

9.	10.
LOOK → **← KOOL**	**SREKROW** **STRIKE**

Brain Tip

Develop a positive mindset and cultivate a happy face—it's an instant face-lift

Brain Bits

Depression is not part of the normal aging process. In many cases, depression is preventable, and it is often reversible.

Develop a positive mind-set. Hone your sense of humor and learn to laugh at yourself and the incongruities of life.

Studies have shown that the healthiest individuals laugh several hundred times a day. A merry heart is good medicine and strengthens brain function and immune-system function.

Studies have also shown that individuals with positive thoughts about aging lived an average of 7.5 years longer than those with negative thoughts about old age.

According to Marcus Aurelius, if you are distressed by anything external, the pain is not due to the thing itself but to your own estimate of it, and this you have the power to revoke at any moment. Your thoughts are one of the few things in life you actually can control.

Chapter Seven

Got My Mojo On…

The human brain is a most unusual instrument of elegant and as yet unknown capacity.
—Stuart Seaton

Go almost anywhere these days and you're sure to find someone talking about needing to be in control, or feeling upset because they aren't in control.

Basically, all you can really control is how and what you think. You may be able to reduce stress and tension by the way you think and by the stories you tell yourself about events that occur.

Brain aerobic puzzles can help you hone mental flexibility. They help to maximize divergent outside-the-box thinking while minimizing convergent inside-the-box thinking.

Inside-the-box thinking is when you review the available information and are expected to arrive at only one conclusion. Honing mental flexibility gives you practice in viewing things from an opposite angle.

You may recall reading that Dr. Edward Jenner solved the smallpox puzzle by studying people who did *not* get the disease. Previous researchers had focused on who *did* get smallpox. That's a great example of out-of-the-box thinking!

Subtract

7 -3	4 -4	10 -5
7 -2	10 - 2	9 -3
9 -8	8 -4	7 -6
7 -7	9 -2	6 -5
4 -1	8 -4	8 -1
5 -4	8 -2	9 -1
15 - 4	18 - 2	17 - 6

Completion Times: ______,

______, ______, ______, ________

A New Wrinkle in My Old Horn

Be careful with these word problems.
All is not as it seems!

1. I have two U.S. coins that add up to fifty-five cents. One is not a half dollar. What coins are they?

2. A boy had nine cats, and all but seven died. How many did he have left?

3. Three large wrestlers try to crowd under one small umbrella, but nobody gets wet. How is this possible?

4. A certain five-letter word becomes shorter when you add two letters to it. What is the word?

5. An electric train is traveling northeast at 75 miles per hour and the wind is blowing southeast at 75 miles per hour. In which direction does the smoke blow?

6. Some months have 30 days and some months have 31 days. How many months have 28 days?

7. Two girls were born to the same mother on the same hour, the same day, and the same year but were not twins. How is this possible?

8. A man lives in a square house where each side has a window with a southern exposure. One morning the man sees a bear walking by. What color is the bear?

9. A man was born in 1975 and died in 1995 at the age of 35. How is this possible?

10. What two words contain the most letters?

11. A 10-volume encyclopedia sits on a shelf, in order, spines outward. Each volume contains one thousand pages. Excluding the covers of each volume, how many pages are between the first page of the encyclopedia and the last?

12. What do you call a man who was born in Eureka, raised in San Francisco, and died in Memphis?

13. I raise my right, and you raise your left, I look at you, you look at me. What are you?

14. I have four fingers and one thumb, but I'm not your hand. What am I?

15. My existence is always in debate. I can't be felt, seen, or touched, yet I have my own style of music. What am I?

Spring and Fall

What does your brain perceive first?
Does the position of the figure make a difference?

Outside the Box

Without lifting your pen or pencil from the paper, draw four straight lines that connect all nine dots. Avoid going back over any of the lines.

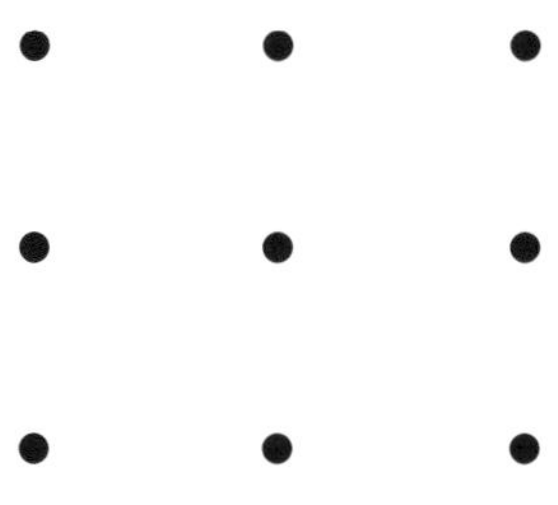

Between You, Me, and the Fence Post

In each puzzle, some clues to a scenario are given, but the clues don't tell the full story. Fill in the details and complete the story. One solution is typically more satisfying than the others.

1. A man marries twenty women but isn't charged with polygamy.

2. A man is alone on an island with no bathroom and no food, yet he does not fear for his life.

3. Bruce wins the race, but he gets no ribbons.

4. A train pulls into a station, but none of the waiting passengers move.

5. A man rides into town on Thursday. He stays three nights and leaves on Thursday.

6. A writer with an audience insisted that he was never to be interrupted while writing. A student interrupted him and he never wrote again.

7. One is sitting down and will never get up. The second eats as much as is given to him, yet is always hungry. The third goes away and never returns. Name each of the three.

8. How many times does the number "9" appear in the sequence of numbers 1-99?

9. I am a three-digit number. My second digit is four times more than my third digit. My first digit is seven less than my second digit. What number am I?

10. The person who invented me doesn't want me personally. The person who buys me doesn't usually need me personally. The one who actually needs me doesn't know it. What am I?

11. You can drop me from the tallest building and I will not break. But if you drop me in the ocean I become unusable. What am I?

12. In which American state is it legal for a widow's husband to marry his wife's sister?

13. An archeologist wrote a paper claiming to have found a coin dated 33BC. How would the media know whether or not the archeologist was telling the truth?

14. You deliver mail on a regular route of one mile north, one mile south, one mile east, and one mile west. How old is the mail carrier?

15. Two men were playing chess. They played five games and each won the same number of games. In addition, there were no ties. How could this happen?

16. How many birthdays does the average child living in New York have?

17. Take a dozen apples away from 27 cherries and what do you have?

18. In Africa a man who is living in Uganda may never be buried in Kampala. What is the reason?

19. In baseball or softball, how many outs are there in one inning?

20. A man checks into a room and cannot sleep. He makes a phone call, says nothing, and goes right to sleep. How does this happen?

21. An American citizen with no passport visits multiple foreign countries in one day. He is welcomed in each country and leaves each one of his own accord. How can this be?

Did you Know?

There is now good scientific evidence to show that exercising the brain can slow, delay, and protect against age-related decline.

True or False – Lifestyle

By age 80 behavioral choices account almost entirely for a person's overall health and longevity.

Brain Benders 7-1

1.	2.
RIDING	BOOHOOSHAME

3.	4.
XAT LIPTON	SQUARERAUQS SQUARERAUQS

5.	6.
IT TI IT TI	✔ ANNUAL

7.	8.
FACE IT IT	GET IT

9.	10.
H H O O O O JUMP PING S S	G P O I S S S S I O P G

Proverbial Puzzles

In each proverb one letter of each multiple-letter word is replaced with another letter. Figure out the original proverb.

1. I sad haid das
2. O tay lane ant o tollar dhort
3. I diasond on tho sough
4. E sace onsy o dother coutd sove
5. Take hat white she sin whines
6. I date gorse thak deash
7. O sool tnd hes koney ate doon farted
8. I sriend on seed as I fkiend inseed
9. Sengend on kis oln nime
10. I san's hot do to fhat o dan's sot do to
11. O penky dor sour thoukht
12. Het swile tee hetting's food

True or False – Education

People who are better educated tend to stay younger longer. Stimulation to the brain through education helps to build more brain tissue.

Hands and More Hands

How many hands and how many
different shapes does your brain perceive?

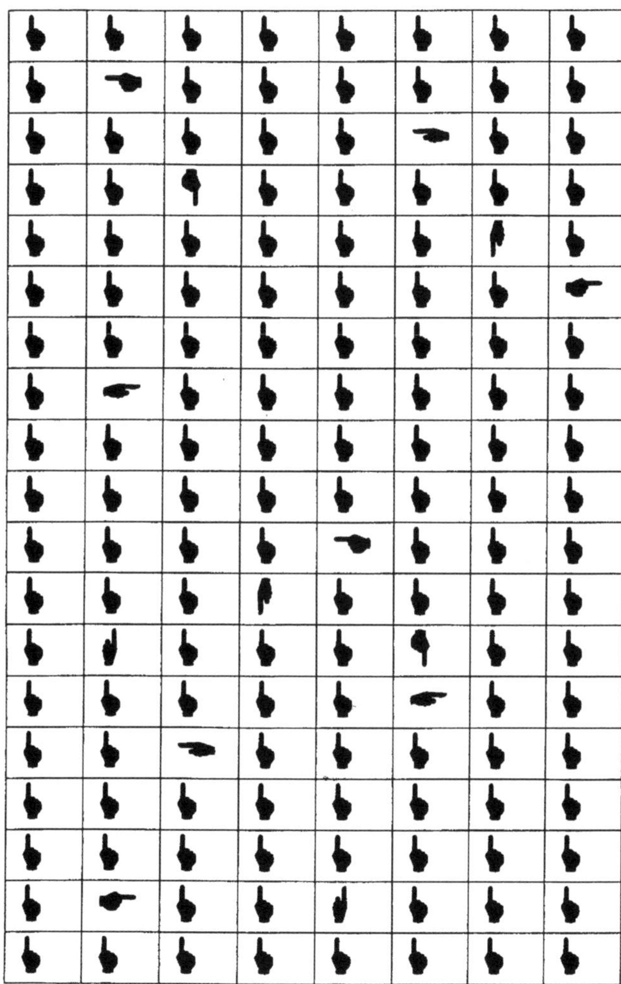

Brain Tip

Exercise daily to keep your brain and body in the best possible condition

Brain Bits

Aerobic exercises are designed to increase breathing and heart rate for an extended period of time (e.g., at least fifteen minutes at a time).

Reported benefits include:

- Helps the brain *boot up* more efficiently
- Increases blood flow to the brain
- Washes away toxins and wastes
- Increases resilience to stress
- Improves creativity and concentration
- Increases levels of serotonin and endorphins
- Helps to stabilize blood sugar levels
- Stimulates the production of neurotrophins (food for the neurons)

The possible cardiovascular benefits are associated with long-term regular exercise. If you are unable to engage in aerobic exercise, work with your physician or healthcare practitioner to do whatever you can. Something is better than nothing!

Chapter Eight

Keep Your Eyes Peeled...

Visualize this thing you want.
See it, feel it, believe in it.
Make your mental blueprint and begin.
—Robert Collier

Visualization is a label for internal mental picturing. You may be more familiar with the phrase *in your mind's eye*, although both terms really mean the same thing and refer to a natural brain phenomenon.

The brain has a built-in ability to recall and reconstruct visual images inside your head when you are in a basic thinking mode.

The brain is also capable of actively creating a visual representation of something you have never actually seen but are creating in your own mind.

Imagining something in your brain is much the same as perceiving it in the real world.

The right hemisphere is strengthened through the use of visualization exercises. When you also stimulate the left hemisphere by engaging in verbal language-based exercises, integration of the two cerebral hemispheres is enhanced.

Book Worms

Does your brain perceive the book as pointing toward or away from you?

True or False – Enculturation

After birth the brain wires up differently in different cultures. Even the brain's visual systems do not develop in exactly the same way.

For example, people who grow up in forests lack depth perception that others, who grew up in different environments, possess. You can remake yourself in adulthood to some degree, but can never totally abandon your early cultural conditioning.

Brain Benders 8-1

1.	2.
B U L L B U L L	LA L NWOT L AL

3.	4.
ELOP	NEVER 1 2 3 4 5 6 7 8 9 10 11 <u>12</u>

5.	6.
EYE	INFIN EVITI

7.	8.
DNUORG 72 INCHES	Π

9.	10.
NOW<u>H</u>ERE	D <u>A</u> Y

Did You Know?

Your habitual attitudes form neural circuits in the brain. If you choose to maintain a specific attitude (e.g., positive mind set), the brain can literally rewire itself to facilitate that attitude.

Can't Take My Eyes off of You

Where does your brain locate the opening to the box? Does the box position make a difference in what your brain perceives?

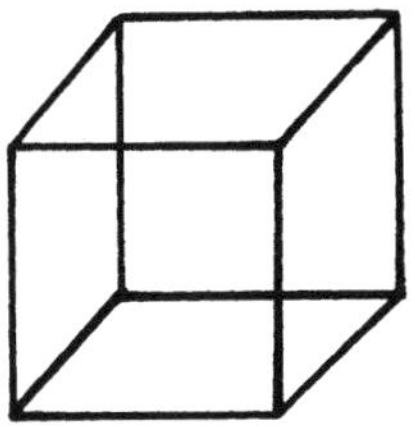

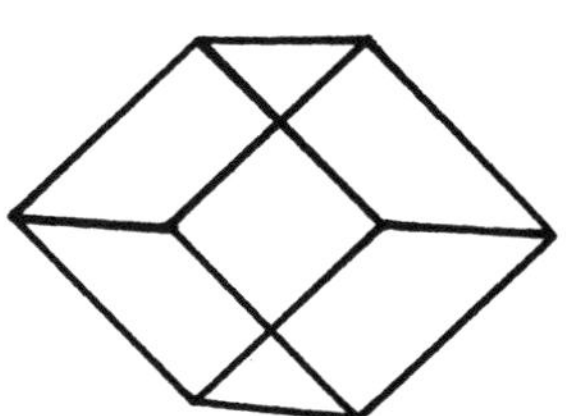

True or False – Sensibility

Vision is the best understood of all the human senses.

True or False – Mmm-m-m-m

The retina in the female brain typically contains more "M" cells, designed to detect motion. The retina of the male brain typically contains more "P" cells, designed to detect color and texture.

Eye Opening

Does your brain find it easier or more difficult to locate openings in this set of figures as compared to those on the previous page?

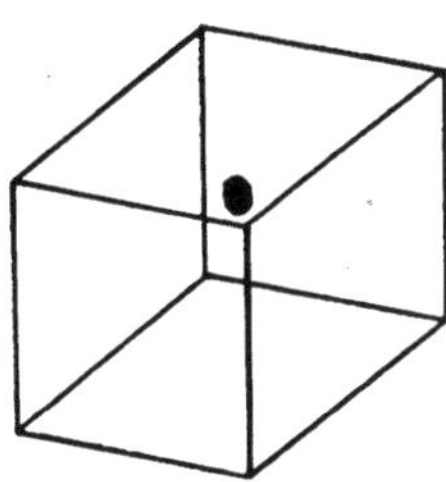

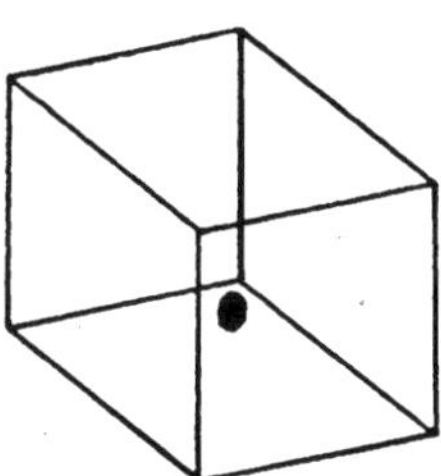

Did You Know?

Adopting healthier lifestyle habits can help to prevent or treat many of the things that can go wrong with the brain.

Brain Benders 8-2

1.	2.
T 2222 44 T	**S M O T A**
3.	**4.**
BCLOUCUSCE	**CHANGEGNAHC**
5.	**6.**
R C O I N Z A I	**R A C A A C A R**
7.	**8.**
TAC A CAT A TAC	**H A R E S**
9.	**10.**
♥ HEAD ♥ ♥ SLEEH ♥	**TYME HANDNAH**

Cubic Synfonia

How many cubes does your brain count?

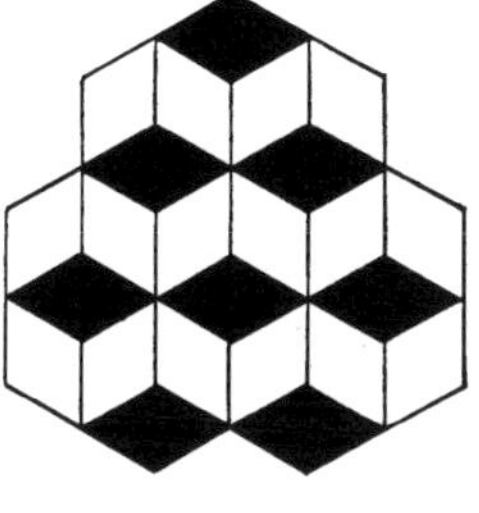

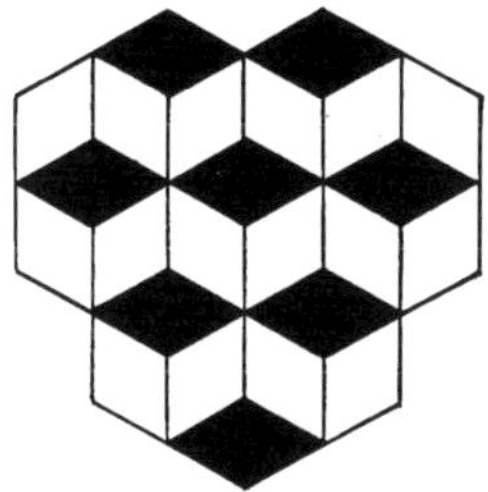

Did You Know?

Males tend to have a narrow, long-range vision style, almost like having a set of built-in binoculars.

This means that the male may find it easier to see items that are a longer distance away (e.g., highway and freeway signs, markers, big-game quarry).

Daffynitions

Match the following unusual definitions
by filling in the blanks

__ Cesarean Section	1. Study of fine paintings
__ Outpatient	2. Lower than the day rate
__ Organic	3. A doctor's walking stick
__ Protein	4. An old spouse or partner
__ Serology	5. One who works on organs
__ Paralyze	6. Person who has fainted
__ Nitrate	7. Die not believing in a deity
__ Morbid	8. A clumsy ophthalmologist
__ Diagnostic	9. English knighthood study
__ Adenoid	10. A higher offer
__ Medical staff	11. One who likes young people
__ Artery	12. A district in Rome
__ Stalemate	13. A couple of untruths
__ Eyedropper	14. Bothered by commercials

__ Dilate	15. What bullfighters do
__ Barium	16. A letter carrier
__ Colic	17. To help a friend relax
__ GI series	18. Gardener does to hedge
__ Hangnail	19. When CPR fails
__ Post-operative	20. To take up your time
__ Vein	21. Break fluid
__ Intravenous	22. Games between soldiers
__ Avoidable	23. Lassie
__ Intense	24. A punctuation mark
__ Eclipse	25. To live longer
__ Coffee	26. Very friendly
__ Belong	27. Where campers sleep
__ Rubberneck	28. Inflated opinion of oneself
__ Coma	29. A goddess enters
__ Congenital	30. A coat hook

Your Favorite Flower

Recall your favorite flower.

- Where did you first see it?
- Does it come in more than one color?
- Does it have a distinctive fragrance?
- In what type of location does it grow best?
- Is it considered a popular flower by florists?
- What does it feel like when you touch it?
- Did you ever receive it as a gift?
- Can you grow it in your garden?
- What memories does it bring to mind?
- What makes it your favorite?

Did You Know?

Females tend to have a short-range peripheral vision style. Typically it is easier for a female to find a specific item in the refrigerator, on a shelf, or in a drawer or cupboard. This may be because her short-range peripheral vision tends to take in more of the immediate environment.

Proof, Proof, What a Goof

How many times does the letter "F" occur in the following paragraph? Which style is easier for your brain to read?

ALL FINISHED FILES ARE THE RESULT OF YEARS OF SCIENTIFIC STUDY COMBINED WITH THE EXPERIENCE OF MANY YEARS, ALONG WITH THE EXPERTISE OF MULTIPLE RESEARCHERS AFFILIATED WITH A MYRIAD OF DIFFERENT SCHOOLS AND UNIVERSITIES.

All finished files are the result of years of scientific study combined with the experience of many years, along with the expertise of multiple researchers affiliated with a myriad of different schools and universities.

True or False – On Board

Learning something *new* stimulates the growth of dendrites, the thousands of shorter projections on each neuron. Challenging your brain on a regular basis makes it more likely that your brain will store new information in long-term memory.

Brain Tip

Anticipate retaining your memory and affirm daily that you are recalling needed information in a timely manner

Brain Bits

Temporary misplacement of stored facts occurs at any age. It is the stories you tell yourself about that temporary misplacement that make all the difference in the world. Some believe one of the biggest contributors to loss of recall is the person expects to lose his/her memory. Ouch!

Avoid saying silently or aloud that you "can't remember." The brain is only too willing to help you follow through on what it perceives you want. Use affirmations to program your subconscious into believing you are retaining recall abilities.

Regularly use brain aerobic exercises to help preserve brain function. It appears there are limits to what the brain can memorize by rote and store. However, the brain appears to possess an unlimited capacity for learning concepts, processing ideas, and putting information together in a new way.

The good news is that intelligent/creative memory can strengthen with age. Remember that and work with it!

Chapter Nine

A Diamond Is Forever…

I'm very pleased with each advancing year. It stems back to when I was forty. I was a bit upset about reaching that milestone, but an older friend consoled me. "Don't complain about growing old; many, many people do not have that privilege."
—Chief Justice Earl Warren

People often miss a great deal in life because they aren't paying attention, or their brain is tired from lack of sleep, or they aren't interested in whatever is happening.

Sometimes they miss information because it relates to what they take in through their eyes, but their sensory preference is auditory or kinesthetic rather than visual. The brain aerobics puzzles in this chapter are designed to help you pay attention and notice differences.

If your sensory preference is visual, these puzzles may be like falling off the proverbial log, and your brain will perceive it is "smart." If your sensory preference is auditory or kinesthetic, identifying the differences may be more of a challenge.

Be persistent! Have fun in the process, and soon you may be crafting your own puzzles and sharing them with family and friends.

Diamonds and More

Count the differences

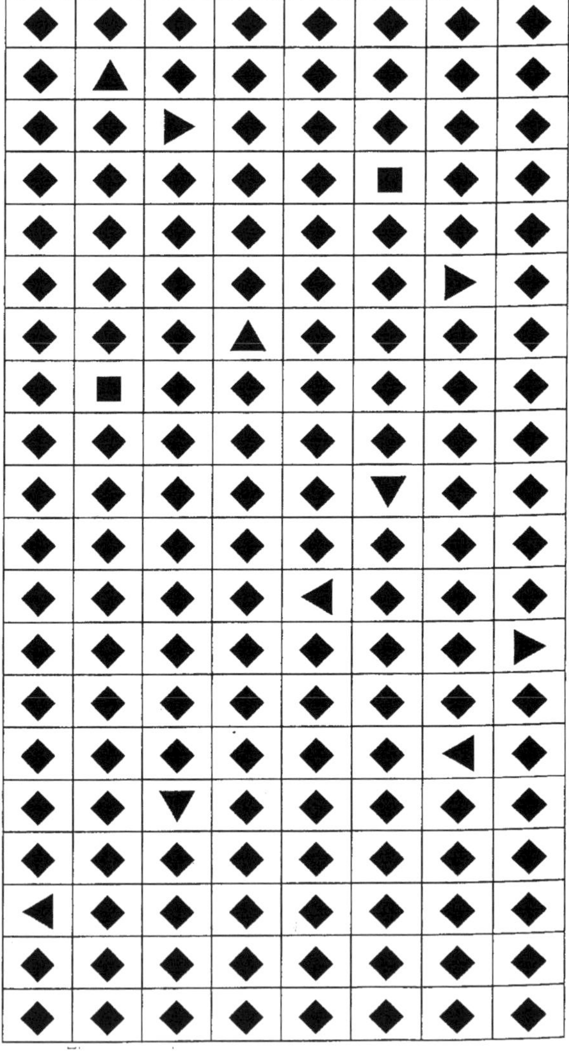

Brain Benders 9-1

<table>
<tr><td>1.

S
T
O
R
Y</td><td>2.

C
A
B
C
A
B</td></tr>
<tr><td>3.

SRUOH OPEN</td><td>4.

GUN JR</td></tr>
<tr><td>5.

POTS
$0.10</td><td>6.

OR 0
OR</td></tr>
<tr><td>7.

SP E
E CH</td><td>8.

AYE
THGIE</td></tr>
<tr><td>9.

TATAT
TIT
TATAT</td><td>10.

L
O
V
E V O L</td></tr>
</table>

Exercise Equipment

Complete the puzzle so that the required letters are used only once in every 3-by-3 box, every row, and every column: BRAIN GYMS

	B		S		A		G	
S	R	A				Y	M	B
			B	Y	M			
		B		M		R		I
R	A		N	B	I		Y	
		I		A		N		S
			A	I	R			
Y	I	N				A	S	R
	G		Y		N		I	

Shorthand Sequences

Fill in the blanks

A-1, D-4, H-8, L ___,

___ 16, T-20

I Knew That!

Answer the following questions.

1. The largest word in the English language?
2. What do you have if an ax falls on your truck?
3. What animal is most likely to break the law?
4. How does an octopus prepare for war?
5. How long did the Hundred Years War last?
6. Which country makes Panama hats?
7. What does a dog get when it graduates from obedience school?
8. What is known to be the loudest sport?

All in a Whirl

How does your brain perceive these figures?
Draw some of your own.

True or False – All Heart

The brain needs about the same amount of blood as does the heart.

Brain Benders 9-2

<table>
<tr><td>1.
AFF4AIRS</td><td>2.
FAN C</td></tr>
<tr><td>3.
W R I T E
R   T
I   I
T   R
E T I R W</td><td>4.
BAR
R
E
<u>L</u></td></tr>
<tr><td>5.
SPUDSPOUND</td><td>6.
FAEULBCE</td></tr>
<tr><td>7.
APPLE</td><td>8.
T T T T T 1</td></tr>
<tr><td>9.
EXPECTATION
NOITATCEPXE
EXPECTATION</td><td>10.
PERSONAL

N</td></tr>
</table>

It's Time

Count the differences

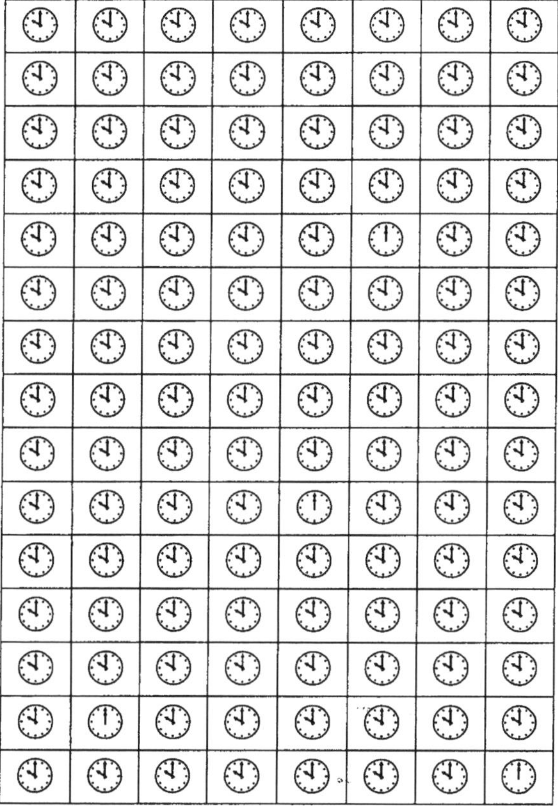

Did You Know?

Time is processed past to future from the back of the brain to the front.

Four and Seven Make Eleven

Move just two lines and create seven squares.

Merry-Go-Round

Can you figure out the reason? Some letters are above the line while others are below. No math is involved.

A E F H I K L M N T V W X Y Z

B C D G J O P Q R S U

Bolts from the Blue

Solve the following riddles.

1. I usually stay in one corner but can go around the world. What am I?

2. Put me in a bucket and I will make it lighter. I am weightless but you can see me. What am I?

3. Until I am measured I am unknown, and yet I am missed when I have flown. What am I?

4. I am always hungry. I eat as much as I am given and yearn for more. What am I?

5. What does a miser spend, a spendthrift save, and all carry to their grave?

6. I can glide though I have no wings, and I can weep though I have no eyes. What am I?

7. Some remains when you take away the whole. What am I?

8. If you break me I still keep on going. If you touch me I may react, but if you lose me nothing will matter. What am I?

9. I lead eternity and bring up the back of time and space. I can be found at the beginning of every end and at the end of every place. What am I?

It's in the Directions

Count the differences

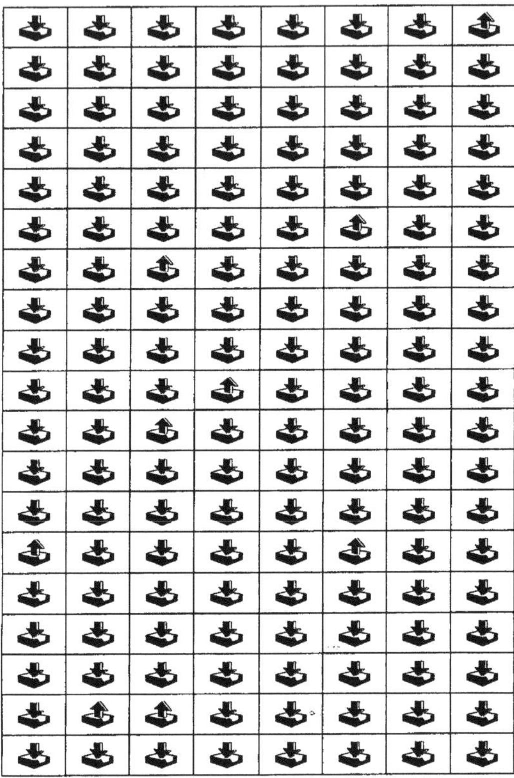

True or False – Lost

Women tend to rely on landmarks and signs to find their way around, while men use distances and directions.

Help Us All!

Answer the following questions and riddles.

1. You can catch me, sometimes quite easily, but I can't be thrown. What am I?

2. Give me food and I thrive. Give me water and I die. What am I?

3. What weighs nothing but is as big as an elephant?

4. If the clock's hour hand moves 1/60 of a degree every minute, how many degrees does it move in one hour?

5. What do you put in a toaster?

6. Avoid using a calculator: You are driving a baseball team from San Francisco to Los Angeles. At stop number seven, eight players get on the bus. At the next stop, five players get off the bus and seven get on. At the following stop three people get off and five get on. At the next to the last stop five people get on and seven get off. You arrive in Boston and thank your driver, whose name is ______________.

7. New York and Paris both have city islands. Which one is on a river?

8. What is the tallest building in the world?

Brain Tip

Eat nutritious meals at regular times, using foods that are in as natural a state as possible

Brain Bits

The brain consumes more energy than any other body organ. It utilizes approximately one fifth of all your energy, 20% of the oxygen you inhale, and 20% of the energy you derive from the food you eat.

It takes energy to digest food. Many waste energy by overeating and deposit the excess to their waist.

Pay attention to what you eat, how much you eat, when you eat, the quality of your food, and your mind-set while you are eating.

- Make certain you give your brain the quality nutrition it needs

- Eat slightly smaller portions at each meal, and reduce your intake of refined sugars and saturated fats

- Select foods and beverages with care—aim for a low-fat, low-salt, high-fiber, and nutritional-product-enhanced diet

Chapter Ten

Time to Bite the Bullet…

The Brain: an apparatus
with which we think we think.
—Ambrose Bierce

Most behaviors, from talking to gesturing or walking, involve some type of motor function, ranging from simple to complex.

However, a *simple* movement like reaching out to pick up a glass of water is actually a *complex* motor task.

First your brain must determine which muscles to contract and in what sequence in order to steer your hand to the glass. Then it must estimate the force needed to pick up the glass and the amount of strength required to hang onto it. The weight, material, and contents of the glass also influence the brain's calculations.

Although there are computers on planet earth that can replicate functions of the brain's left hemisphere (and do them faster and sometimes more accurately than the average human brain), there is not yet a computer that can duplicate all the functions of the brain's right hemisphere.

Use the following puzzles to challenge both sides of your brain.

Text Messages

Complete the puzzle so that the required numbers and symbols are used only once in every 3-by-3 box, every row, and every column: **1 2 3 4 5** ⓧ Ⓡ Ⓒ Ⓟ

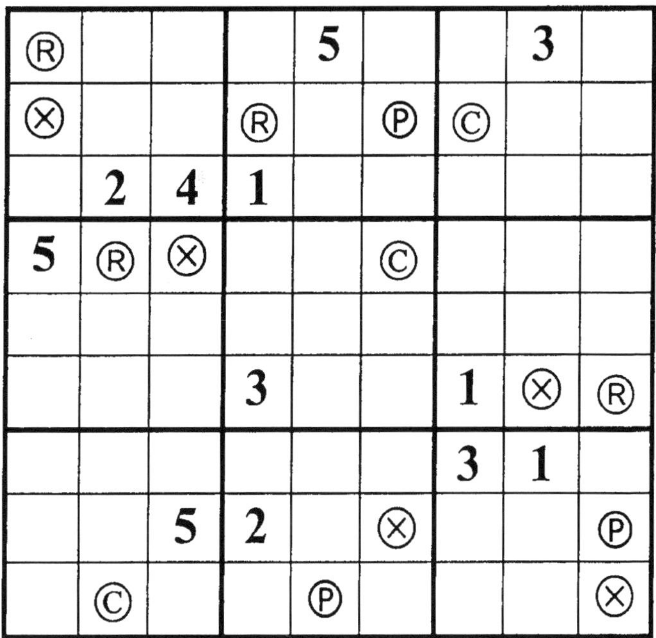

Ⓡ				5			3	
ⓧ			Ⓡ		Ⓟ	Ⓒ		
	2	4	1					
5	Ⓡ	ⓧ			Ⓒ			
			3			1	ⓧ	Ⓡ
						3	1	
		5	2		ⓧ			Ⓟ
	Ⓒ			Ⓟ				ⓧ

True or False – Nimble Thimble

The brain's nimbleness in accessing words instantly can decline with age. On the flip side, your vocabulary can improve with age.

You've Got to be Joking!

Figure out the answers to the following questions.

1. What's the difference between a locomotive engineer and a teacher?
2. What key in music makes a good army officer?
3. A ballerina drives what type of truck?
4. What kind of artist can't you trust?
5. An electrician drives what type of car?
6. What animal uses a nutcracker?
7. What do you call a dog that is left-handed?
8. What do you call a dog with no legs?
9. What do you get if you cross two young dogs with a pair of earplugs?
10. What is the difference between a fisherman and a lazy student?
11. What is the difference between a gardener and a billiard player?
12. What is the difference between a jeweler and a jailer?

Arrows and More

Complete the puzzle so that the required numbers and symbols are used only once in every 3-by-3 box, every row, and every column: 1 ↑ 3 ↓ 5 → 7 ← 9

	3				→			1
↑							3	
7			5	3				
				1		9		
			9		3		7	
←		9						3
				7	9			
	9							↓
							5	

True or False – Yours or Mine

Memories have been instilled in your cells. If you receive someone else's cells, you may receive the memories that were encoded in those cells.

Multiply

6 x3	2 x2	10 x8
7 x3	10 x6	9 x5
9 x6	8 x3	7 x4
7 x5	9 x7	6 x6
9 x4	8 x7	7 x6
7 x3	9 x9	6 x4
9 x3	9 x7	9 x4

Completion Times: ______,

______, ______, ______, _______

Ring Around the Rosy

Count the differences

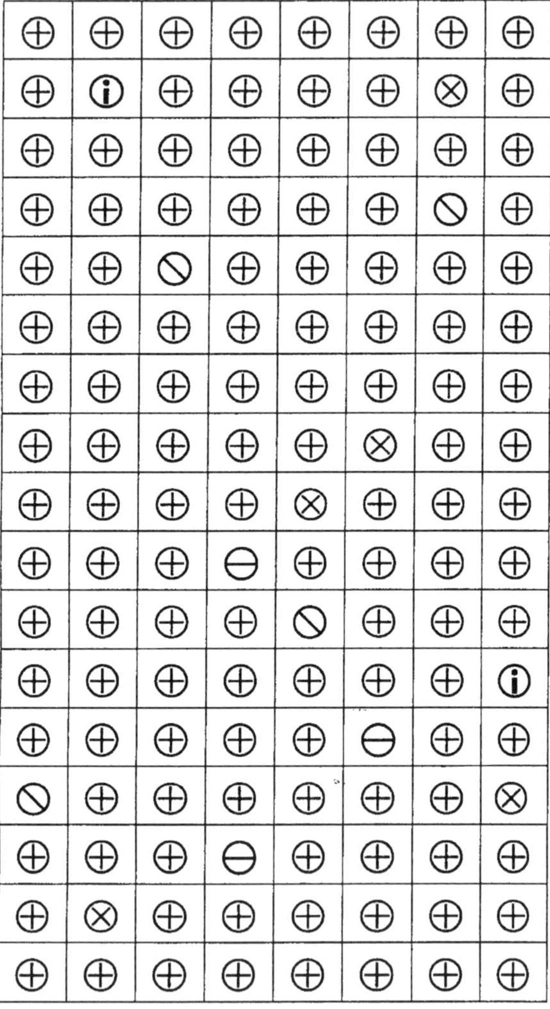

Double Dog Dare

Fill in the blanks to complete the sayings.

1. A penny saved is a penny _________
2. Home is where the ___________ is
3. A stitch in time saves ______________
4. You are never too old to _____________
5. A fool and his ___________ are soon parted
6. A heart as big as _______________
7. A little _____________told me
8. A little __________ is a dangerous thing
9. After the feast comes the ____________
10. Never give a __________ a break
11. Moving at a ___________ pace
12. Older than _______________
13. One _______________short of a load
14. One ________in the _______
15. Proof is in the _____________
16. Pulled on like an old ________
17. Ran like a ____________ dog
18. A rolling ______________ gathers no moss
19. Scared out of my _________________
20. Screaming like a _______________
21. _________, not _________, leads to fortune

22. Slick as a bucket of ________________
23. You can't get blood out of a _________
24. Afraid of one's own _____________
25. Sure as __________ follows __________
26. A chain is as strong as its weakest _____
27. Add __________ to the fire
28. As a ______ is bent the ______ will grow
29. All's ______ that ends _______
30. Get your _____ out of the ______
31. Not working with a full ________
32. A _______ worse than death
33. A _______ in the hand is worth _______
34. A man of few __________
35. A play on _____________
36. There's a method in his _________
37. ___________in the oven
38. A _________ in your cap
39. After all is said and _________
40. Cost an _________ and a _________
41. Footloose and _______________ free
42. Have a __________ to stand on
43. Knee-high to a _________________
44. Makes one's __________ curl

It's More than Water

Complete the puzzle so that the required letters are used only once in every 3-by-3 box, every row, and every column: MIND WAVES

N		V		W		I		A
	D			I			N	
W		A		N		E		M
D		S	N		I	A		W
			D	V	W			
V		W	A		M	D		N
E		M		D		N		S
	A			M			E	
I		N		A		M		D

Did You Know?

Working (short-term) memory is involved in all aspects of thinking and problem solving (e.g., you can read a menu and retain options in your mind while listening to the specials). It accommodates one task at a time. That is, a new task tends to bump out the content of the old task.

Squares and More Squares

Count the squares

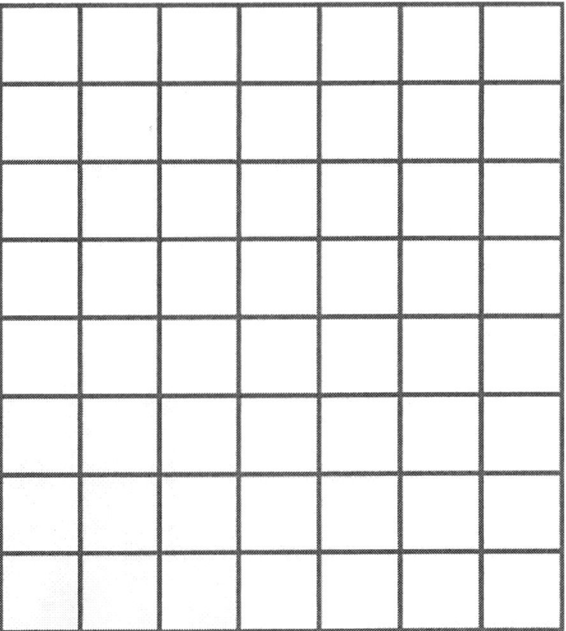

Did You Know?

The average number of things you can keep active in working/short-term memory at the same time is about seven. That's enough for you to be able to read a telephone number and recall the numbers while you dial or otherwise enter the numbers into your phone.

Brain Benders 10-1

<table>
<tr><td>1.

MOMIRRORSOR</td><td>2.

CLOCK
LLAW</td></tr>
<tr><td>3.

T T T T T T
T T T</td><td>4.

KOOB
SHELF</td></tr>
<tr><td>5.

RAEW
LONG</td><td>6.

EWE
EXTENDED</td></tr>
<tr><td>7.

THOUTSOLGHT</td><td>8.

GRTOOFAVE</td></tr>
<tr><td>9.

MOR<u>N</u>ING</td><td>10.

SHOULDER$_0$</td></tr>
</table>

True or False – Altogether now

Deep-breathing techniques can help quiet the mind while they energize the body and brain.

Brain Tip

Make caring for your brain part of your daily routine

Brain Bits

As mentioned in the *Preface – Wet Your Whistle,* information abounds about ways in which you can care for your brain. Brain breathing is one of them. Another is making sure to eat breakfast.

According to Gary Small, MD, author of *The Memory Bible,* eating breakfast increases blood sugar levels and leads to greater mental clarity during the day.

- Studies of elementary school students showed they had improved academic performance and behaviors when they ate breakfast.

- Studies of adults who ate breakfast showed they maintained higher blood sugar levels, had quicker recall, and exhibited better overall memory performance than those who skipped it.

In his book, Immune Power, Jon D. Kaiser, MD, indicates that Indicates that breakfast is the most important meal of the day. Help your brain boot-up by starting each day with a healthy breakfast!

Chapter Eleven

Make a Short Story Long…

When I was young I could remember everything, whether it happened or not. Now that I am older I can remember only those things that never happened.
—Mark Twain

"I don't remember!" Sound familiar? "Benign Senescence" is the term for a type of age-related forgetfulness that happens to most people. It takes energy for the brain to "store" and to "recall" information. Therefore, a tired brain may have more difficulty with forgetfulness at any age.

The good news is that you have partial—if not complete—control over many of the factors that impact memory, such as a lack of physical or mental exercise, poor nutrition, unhealthful eating habits, dehydration, high intake of alcoholic beverages, insufficient sleep, insufficient time for relaxation and play, personal laziness, failure to pay attention, and gerotophobia—the fear of aging.

Do what you can to take good care of your brain. You're the only one who can, and you'll only have yourself to thank as you age!

Math is Bustin' Out

What does your brain perceive?

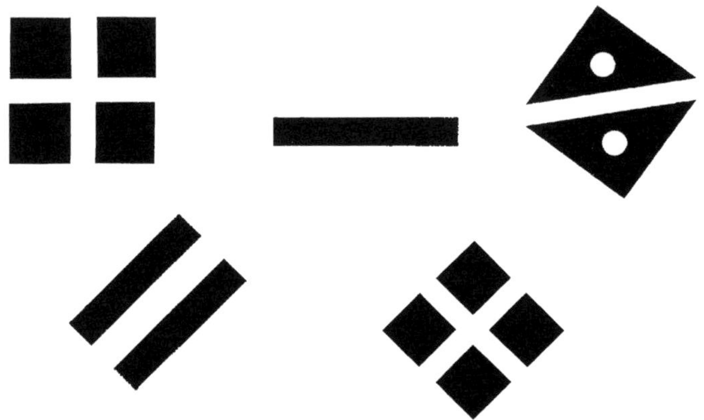

Which Way Out?

What does your brain perceive?

One plus One

Complete the puzzle so that the required letters are used only once in every 3-by-3 box, every row, and every column: TWO BRAINS

W		I	O			A		T
	S		T	N			O	B
T				A		W		
	B			R			I	
O	A	T				R	W	N
		S		W		O		A
B	T			I	N		R	
A		R			T	N		I

True or False – AM or PM

Short-term memory tends to be sharpest in the morning and least effective in the afternoon, while long-term memory is generally best in the afternoon.

It's Miscellani

Complete the puzzle so that the required numbers and symbols are used only once in every 3-by-3 box, every row, and column: 1 ☑ 2 ☒ 3 ⊘ 4 ⊕ 5

⊕				1	4	5		
					⊘		⊕	
			☒	5		☑	1	
3		⊕					4	☑
			1		☒			
☒	2							⊕
	4	⊘		☑	3			
	☑		⊘					
		3	2	☒				4

True or False – Banks

Memories are stored only in the cells of the brain.

Brain Benders 11-1

<table>
<tr><td>1.
FAN</td><td>2.
HOTOH
HANDLELDNAH</td></tr>
<tr><td>3.
D
N
E</td><td>4.
D
H L
O RUNNING O
T C</td></tr>
<tr><td>5.
C
O KICKCIK
U
N OFF
T</td><td>6.
L LAF
I ROOF
N
G</td></tr>
<tr><td>7.
BESGUBD</td><td>8.
ORYACHESTLPRA</td></tr>
<tr><td>9.
SHE'S
S'EHS</td><td>10.
———END</td></tr>
</table>

Ain't Just Waltzing Around

Solve the following riddles.

1. You will see me only once in a minute, twice in a moment, but never in a thousand years? What am I?

2. When is affection shown by a sea-going vessel?

3. I have never been found in a body of water. What kind of stone am I?

4. You can always count on me if life gets tough. What am I?

5. Many things can create me. I can be of any shape or size. I am created for various reasons, and I can shrink or grow with time. What am I?

6. While waiting to be filled, my tongue hangs out. What am I?

7. No sooner spoken than broken. What am I?

8. I am liquid while being created. If you push me too hard I will break. What am I?

9. At times I appear to be near, other times far. I never went to school, but I speak all languages. What am I?

Clothing – Recall

Did you have a favorite item of clothing in childhood?

- What did it look like?
- How did it feel against your skin?
- What color was it or what type of fabric?
- What happened to it?
- How often do you think about it in adulthood?

Presents – Recall

What was the most special present you
recall receiving in childhood?

- What was the occasion?
- Do you still have it?
- As an adult, have you ever received a gift that equaled its specialness?

Angles and Curves

Fill in the blanks to complete the series.

- A E, F H, ___ K, L ___, N ___
- B C, D G, J ___, P Q, ___ S

Add

1 +6	8 +7	4 +6
3 +6	6 +7	4 +8
9 +6	8 +2	4 +9
7 +4	9 +7	6 +6
9 +9	8 +8	4 +4
9 +7	12 +8	14 +4
7 +5	9 +8	6 +8

Completion Times: ______,

______, ______, ______, ________

Triggering Recall

1. What is your earliest memory?

    ____

2. What was your first car? ____________________

3. What was the name of the street you lived on during childhood? ______________________

4. What was the color of the house in which you grew up? _________________________________

5. What was the name of your best same-sex friend in grade school or middle school?

    ____

6. What was the name of your best opposite-sex friend in grade school or middle school?

    ____

7. What were the names of your two best friends in high school? _____________________________

8. What was your favorite subject in high school?

    ____

9. What is one life lesson you would like to share with the younger generation?

    ____

10. How old were you when you realized there was no Easter Bunny? ____

11. How old were you when you discovered that a friend or parent played Santa Claus? ____

A Warm Glow

List seven favorite childhood memories.

- ______________________________
- ______________________________
- ______________________________
- ____________________________________
- ____________________________________
- ____________________________________
- ____________________________________

True or False – Memories

Long-term survival memories from the first three years of life are thought to be housed in the amygdalae, a pair of tiny brain organs located in the second brain layer (pain-pleasure center).

Brain Benders 11-2

1.	2.
LAMP NO	MUSIC TFOSOFT
3.	**4.**
YLF WALL	HADRIBND
5.	**6.**
BA CKWORK	SAND WICH
7.	**8.**
LAIRTRIAL NOITALUBIRT TRIBULATION	ENGRAVING GOLDNOIC
9.	**10.**
GOINGU	☐ MD

Brain Tip

Create and maintain realistic expectations

Brain Bits

Unrealistic expectations, your own as well as those of others, can get you in trouble in a nanosecond.

Take control of your expectations—they are your brain's mental road map.

Unhelpful expectations can include overemphasizing independence at the expense of interdependence. Learn to accept help graciously when it is offered.

According to Barry Gordon, MD, PhD, intelligent/creative memory strengthens as you call on your memories and the connections among them.

Reminisce regularly, recalling the good times along with the bad; this contributes to successful adjustment in the present.

According to Richard Bandler in his book *Using Your Brain for a Change*, the greatest error of all is in thinking that the only way for you to feel good in certain situations is for someone else to behave in a specific way.

Chapter Twelve

As Luck Would Have It…

No mind should have to beg to differ.
—Mel Levine, MD

All human brains have the same general features and would look quite similar to the naked eye. However, the specific configuration of bumps and fissures along the cortical surface of any individual brain is unique to that brain.

The brain contains about the same number of neurons in each brain system. The way in which those neurons are connected is a distinct reflection of a person's special genetic endowment and life experiences.

Throughout a lifetime, circuit connections are made stronger or weaker according to their use. Since each brain's developmental pattern is unique, no two brains are alike. Even the brains of identical twins differ in structure, function, and perception.

Direct your own brain. Avoid letting it run undirected or be directed by others.

Celebrate the uniqueness of your brain. Honor it. Sharpen it. Age-proof it with brain aerobic exercises!

Happy Days Are Here Again

How many faces and how many
differences does your brain perceive?

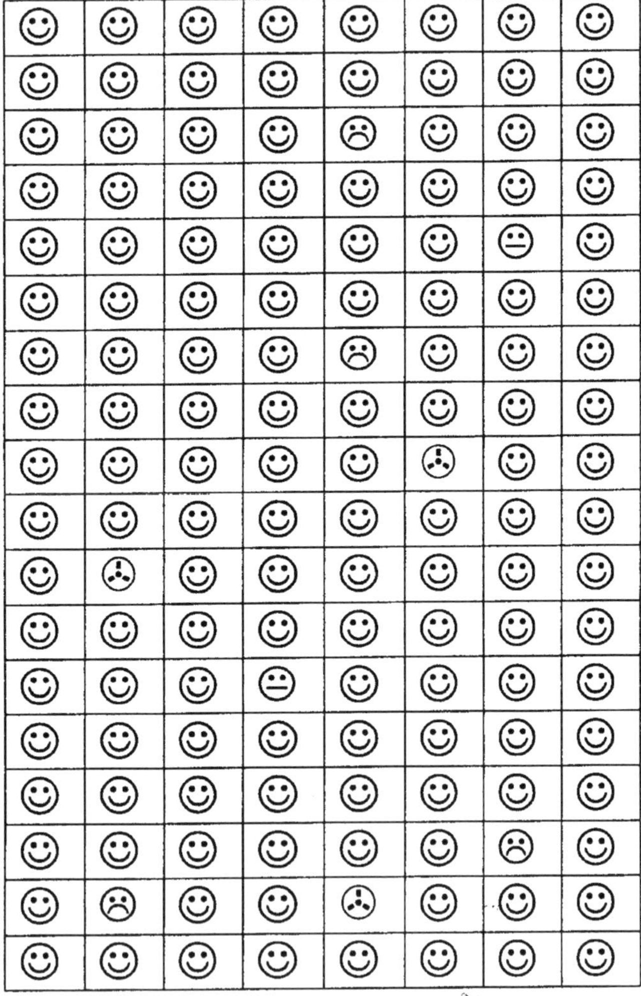

Odd Suits

Complete the puzzle so that the required numbers and symbols are used only once in every 3-by-3 box, every row, and every column: 1 ♦ 3 ♥ 5 ♠ 7 ♣ 9

	3		1	♦	5	7	9	
			♣				♠	♥
1		♦		3				♠
7								5
3				♥		♦		9
♥	7				3			
	♠	3	♦	5	9		♥	

It Happened in Scotland

What is the answer?

As I was going to St. Ives
I met a man with seven sacks
And every sack had seven cats
And every cat had seven kits
How many eyes were going to St. Ives?

Compound Complexity

What does your brain perceive?

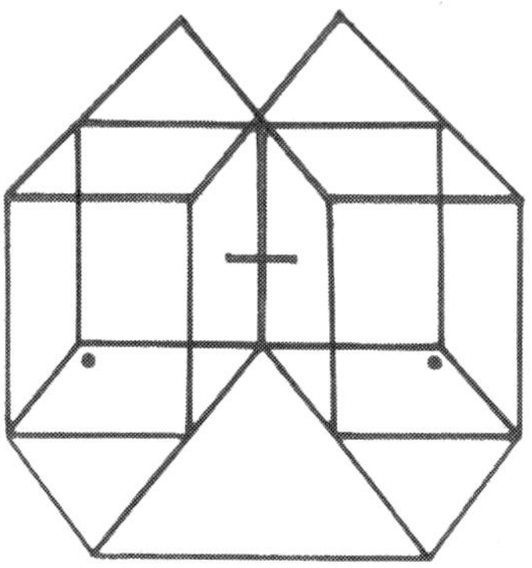

What does your brain perceive when the figure is upside down?

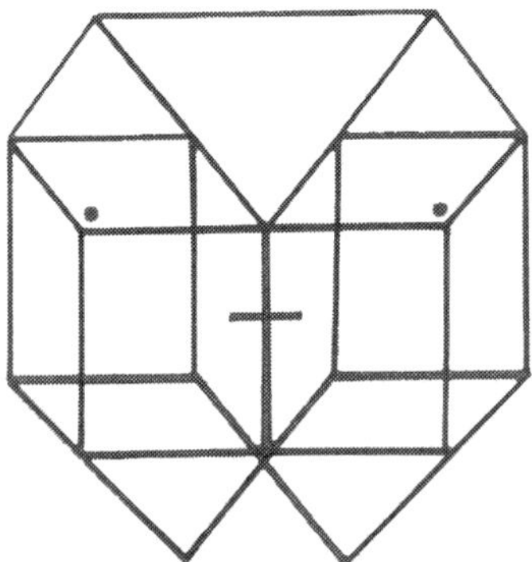

Did You Know?

The brain is one of the most metabolically active organs. In a resting state the brain utilizes 20% or more of the body's total oxygen.

Faces, Faces, and More Faces

What does your brain perceive?

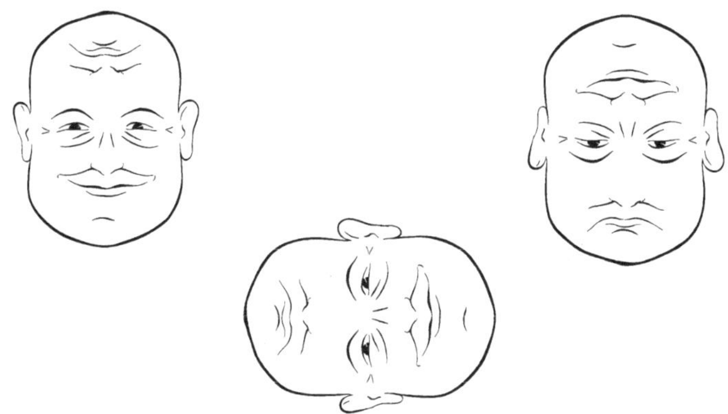

True or False – Real Age

The maximum amount a person can reduce real age (psychological/biological) below his or her actual chronological age is about five years over an entire lifetime.

Multiply

1 x 6	8 x 7	4 x 6
3 x 6	6 x 7	4 x 8
9 x 6	8 x 2	4 x 9
7 x 4	9 x 7	6 x 6
4 x 4	6 x 9	8 x 6
6 x 7	5 x 4	8 x 9
3 x 12	5 x 9	7 x 7

Completion Times: ______,

______, ______, ______, ________

All Heart

Complete the puzzle so that the required letters and symbols are used only once in every 3-by-3 box, every row, and every column: ♥ HEART 🔔 ☆ ✓

E		R				A	🔔	
			R	T		☆		
			H				T	
T	H	E			R			
	🔔						R	
			✓			E	A	T
	♥				H		☆	
		T		R	♥			
	✓	H				🔔		♥

True or False – Funny

Females are socialized to be funny and try harder to be funny than males. In some studies, females were found to be five times funnier as compared to males.

Enigma

What does your brain perceive when you stare at these figures for a few moments?

Did You Know?

Estimates are that more than half of the cells in the heart are actually neurons rather than muscle cells as was previously believed.

These heart neurons appear to function in much the same way as those in the brain, using neurotransmitters, axons, and dendrites.

Heart neurons are thought to provide the basis for emotional intelligence. There is a close two-way connection between the brain and the heart.

Just Checking

Complete the puzzle so that the required letters, number, and symbol are used only once in every 3-by-3 box, every row, and every column: 1 CHEKOUT ✓

1	U					C	O	
	T	O	1	K	H			
					O		H	
		E	H				1	
				T				
	C				1	K		
	E		C					
			E	O	K	1	U	
	O	1					C	✓

True or False – Music

Because all cultures have music, it has been referred to as a universal language. Language cannot exist without a form of music (e.g., melodic speech sounds). Therefore, all people who make speech sounds have the potential for making music.

Brain Benders 12-1

1.	2.
N I 4 N I	**PANTING PUP**
3.	**4.**
C SUN C SUN **NUS C NUS C**	**WORLD** **EHT**
5.	**6.**
TY **LI** **BI** **MO**	**l** **A** **I** **D FRIEND**
7.	**8.**
CON **CON** **CON** **CON**	**E** **A R** **C M** **BA NA NA**
9.	**10.**
SIGH_	**THER_**

Around the Track

Complete the puzzle so that the required letters are used only once in every 3-by-3 box, every row, and every column: BRAIN JOGS

N			S		R	J		
	S			J			N	
		J	I		B			A
		N	G		J	S		O
J	R			B			I	
S		G	R		A	B		N
		B	O		N			J
	J			A			O	
O			J		G	I		

Did You Know?

Aerobic exercise helps the brain boot up efficiently. It also can help raise serotonin levels, increase resilience to stress, decrease hydrocortisone levels, increase blood flow to the frontal cortex, raise levels of free-radical fighters, and trigger the growth of neuron dendrites.

Brain Tip

When you are unable to avoid a negative stressor, apply the 20:80 Rule

Brain Bits

The brain reacts with split-second timing when it recognizes a stressor, instructing the body how to adjust. The brain can stimulate the *stress reaction* for as long as 72 hours after a traumatic incident.

Studies have shown a relationship between stress and aging. The faster you rev your body with stress, the more quickly you age.

Cortisol, a chemical released during episodes of stress, has been found to destroy brain cells, especially in the hippocampus, the brain organ that may be most sensitive to stress.

According to 7th Century Philosopher Epictetus, it's not what happens to you that matters as much as what you think about it.

Sometimes referred to as the 20:80 Rule, this means that while you may not be able to control all events and/or stressors, you *can* control your response to them (the 80%).

Chapter Thirteen

Alive and Kicking...

Aging is not 'lost youth' but a new stage of opportunity and strength.
—Betty Friedan

Neuroplasticity is a term that refers to the brain's ability to grow, adapt, and alter its patterns of connections throughout a lifetime. Even the aging brain is believed to possess this ability. That's an excellent reason for implementing a program of brain aerobic exercises.

Neuroplasticity also means that as you age, you can actually increase the number of connections among neurons. The more you use your brain, the higher the ratio of synapses (connections) to neurons (thinking cells), which can help to delay the onset of symptoms of senility.

Activities that stimulate the senses and engage multiple portions of the brain can help strengthen the mind and retard memory loss. Continually expose your brain to new information.

As you age, your brain can learn new "tricks," but you have to be convinced that you need to learn them. Keep learning!

One for the Money

Complete the puzzle so that the numbers 1-9 are used only once in every 3-by-3 box, every row, and every column.

6			1		8	2		3
	2			4			9	
8		3			5	4		
5		4	6		7			9
	3						5	
7			8		3	1		2
		1	7			9		6
	8			3			2	
3		2	9		4			5

Did You Know?

Creativity is not necessarily making something new. Rather, it may involve a reshuffling of existing facts and ideas. It is a way of seeing things not perceived before. Brainstorming and creativity are compatible brain functions. In fact, brainstorming is actually a subsidiary of creativity.

Brain Benders 13-1

1.	2.
KE O BR	ING NIN WHI

3.	4.
ST E COWPIE	SOARING SESSAM

5.	6.
SONG SONG SONG <u>SONG</u>	S T E I P T

7.	8.
MOUREHSNING	EDUYSTE

9.	10.
WISREHTAEFND	FA L HOLE

Table Top Plates

What does your brain perceive?

The Hand Has It

Which statement does your brain select as likely the most correct overall?

1. A bird in the the hand is worth two in the bush
2. A bird in the hand is worth too in the bush
3. A bird in the hand is is worth two in the bush
4. A bird in the hand is worth to in the bush
5. A bird in the hand could be worth two in the bush—then again, maybe not

True or False – Couch Potato

Movement (e.g., stretching, standing, or marching) does little to combat drowsiness when you are trying to learn.

Little Boxes, Little Boxes

Where does your brain locate the opening to each box? Does the position of the box make a difference?

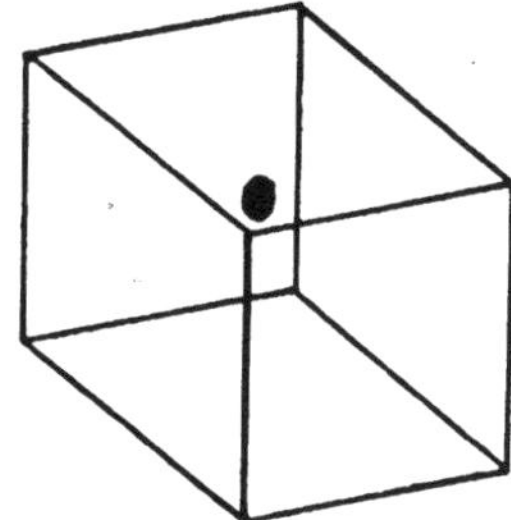

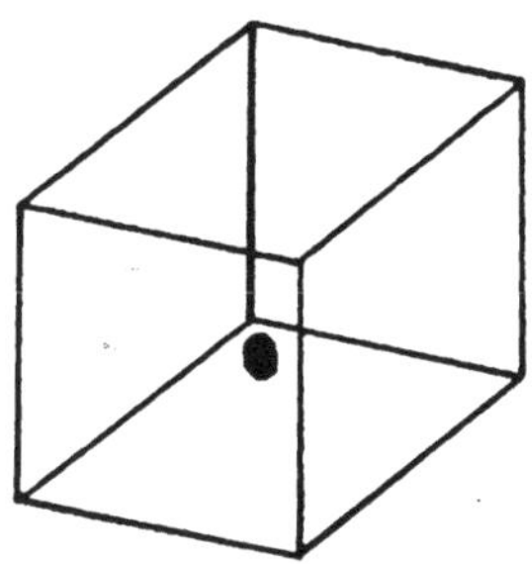

Traveling Light

What is the answer?

Seven tourists were in a bus
And each of them had seven bags
And every bag had seven goats
And every goat had seven kids
How many legs were in the bus?

Two for the Show

Complete the puzzle so that the numbers 1-9 are used only once in every 3-by-3 box, every row, and every column.

		3	9				5	1
5	4	6		1	8	3		
					7	4	2	
				5			3	
2			6		3			4
	8			7		2		
	9	7	3					
		1	8	2		9	4	7
8	5				4	6		

North, South, East, and West

What does your brain perceive?

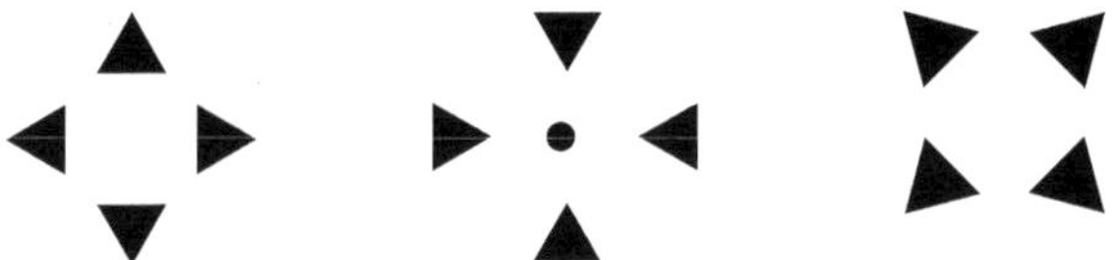

Climbing the Walls

What does your brain perceive?
Does the position of the figure make a difference?

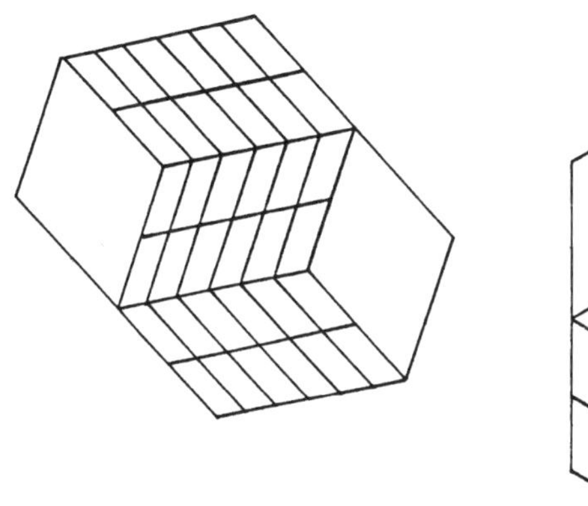

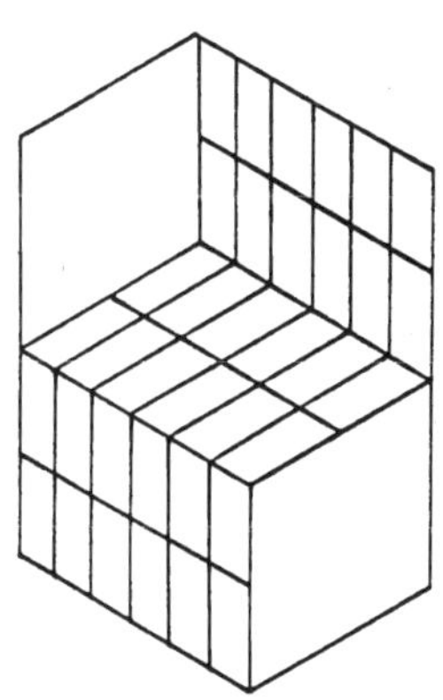

Did You Know?

The brain itself has different levels of vigilance, but it never truly falls completely asleep. Portions of it continue to work during sleep to process information, store memories, and solve problems.

During sleep the subconscious is free to take an unorthodox approach to problem-solving, creativity, insight, you name it.

Add

1 +6	8 +7	4 +6
3 +6	6 +7	4 +8
9 +6	8 +2	4 +9
7 +4	9 +7	6 +6
4 +4	6 +9	8 +6
6 +7	5 +4	8 +9
2 +9	4 +7	5 +9

Completion Times: ______,

______, ______, ______, ______

Three to Get Ready

Complete the puzzle so that the numbers 1-9 are used only once in every 3-by-3 box, every row, and every column.

6		5	7	2			3	9
4					5	1		
	2		1					4
	9			3		7		6
1			8		9			5
2		4		5			8	
8					3		2	
		2	9					1
3	5			6	7	4		8

True or False – Brain Spud

Although not muscles, neurons resemble muscle tissue. Like muscles, neurons strengthen with exercise and wither without it.

Pleasant Potpourri

How many symbols and how many differences does your brain perceive?

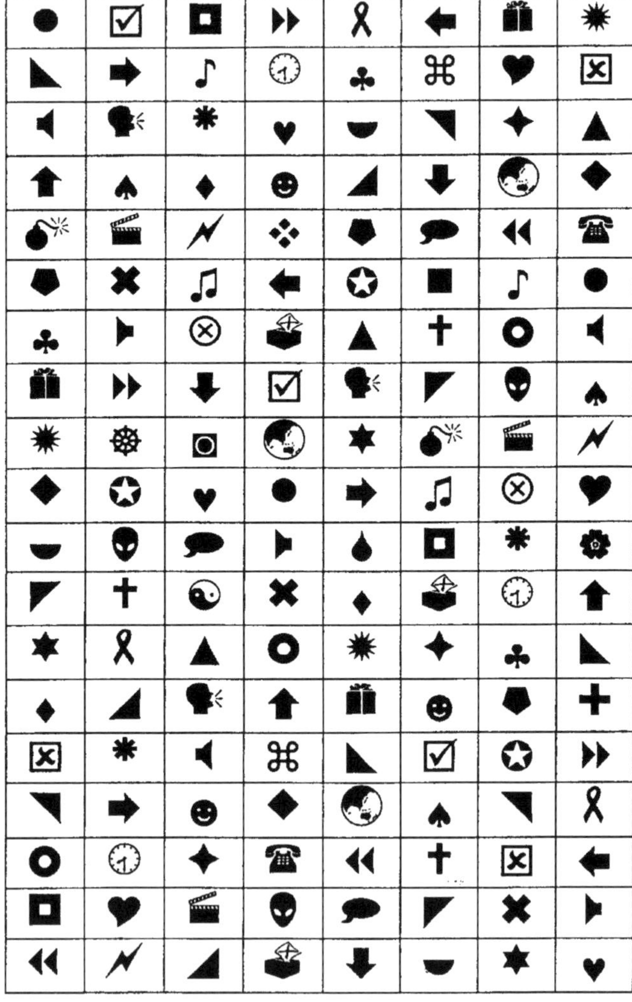

Four to Go

Complete the puzzle so that the numbers 1-9 are used only once in every 3-by-3 box, every row, and every column.

		8		3		5	4	
3			4		7	9		
4	1				8			2
	4	3	5		2		6	
5								8
	6		3		9	4	1	
1			8				2	7
		5	6		3			4
	2	9		7		8		

True or False – Prevention

An optimistic attitude does not help prevent you from getting sick.

Brain Tip

Take responsibility for getting the optimum amount of sleep your brain needs

Brain Bits

Adequate sleep is absolutely essential for brain health. In fact, the brain may require more sleep than the body. It usually takes longer to recover from taxing mental exercise than from physical exercise.

There is an optimum level of sleep for each person: not too much and not too little.

When people get less than the optimal number of hours of sleep, their concentration level is only 70% of what it is on days when they are well-rested.

After 20 hours without sleep, reaction time is similar to a person with a blood alcohol level of 0.08.

It is important to get a good sleep before you learn and after you learn, because learning is enhanced when the brain is well-rested.

According to Dr. Candace Pert, your quality of sleep tends to improve the more closely going to bed and getting up match the natural pattern of night and day.

Chapter Fourteen

More Bang for Your Buck…

Do not worry about your difficulties in mathematics. I can assure you mine are still greater.
—Albert Einstein

Studies have shown that you get more *bang for your buck* when you challenge your brain with simple rather than complex arithmetic problems, and when you continually try to beat your own time for arriving at the answers.

Write your answers to these simple math problems on a separate piece of paper. Time yourself using a watch with a second hand, or a stop watch, or the kindness of a friend to track your time. The goal is to try to reduce the time it takes for you to answer a given set of simple arithmetic problems.

To keep your brain interested, vary the type of arithmetic exercises. This can help to challenge different brain functions. Rotate among addition, subtraction, multiplication, and division problems.

When you've mastered the puzzles in this chapter, create some of your own and exchange them with friends.

Brain Benders 14-1

1.	2.
DOOLB **HANDS**	**BANANA**
3.	**4.**
DISH	**F E** **I CANDLE R** **R I** **E F**
5.	**6.**
NURSES **EKIRTS**	**KNEKAEWES**
7.	**8.**
ANG **ABOLO** **NGOLOB** **BOLOGNA**	**N** **I** **G** **H** **T**
9.	**10.**
COLLAPSE **DEB**	**P.M. A.M.**

Subtract

6 -3	2 -2	10 -8
7 -3	10 -6	9 -5
9 -6	8 -3	7 -4
7 -5	9 -7	6 -6
4 -4	8 -5	8 -6
9 -4	8 -6	9 -9
12 -5	9 -5	8 -5

Completion Times: ______,

______, ______, ______, _______

It's in the Curls

Count the differences

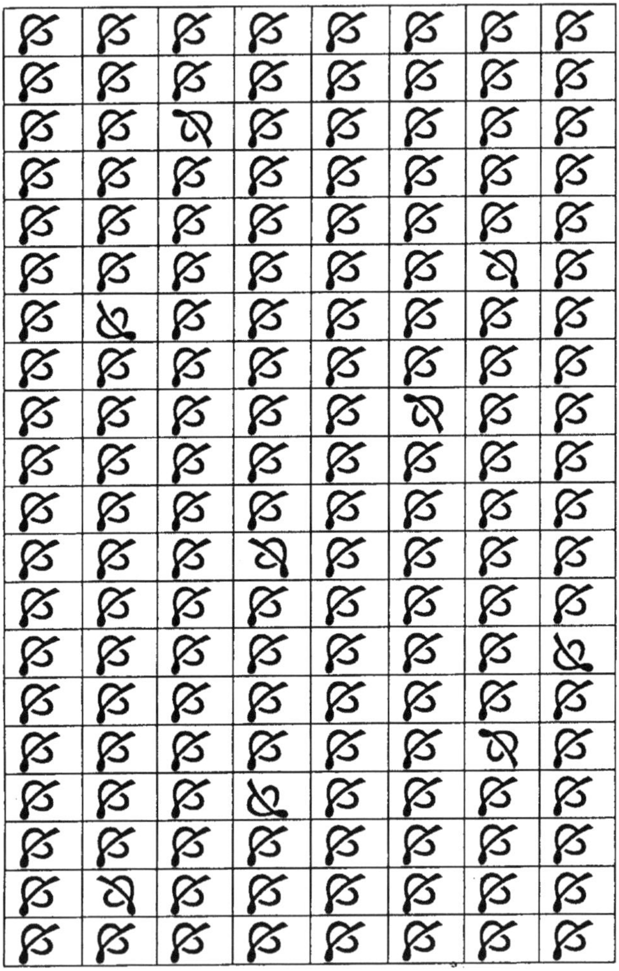

Upstairs Downstairs

What does your brain perceive? Does the direction in which the stairs face make any difference?

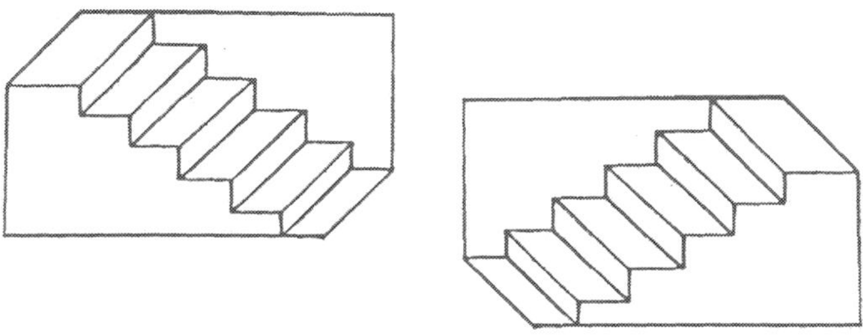

Favorite Toy – Recall

Recall your favorite toy. Did you like it because of how it felt, sounded, looked, or moved? Has it impacted the toys you have given to others? Tell someone a story about your favorite toy.

Favorite Pet – Recall

Recall your favorite pet or someone else's pet you knew well. Did you like it because of the way it looked, sounded, or felt? How did it respond to you? What is your most important pet memory? Tell someone a story about your favorite pet.

Frames Have It

Count the differences

Think Again Twice

Solve the following riddles.

1. A diner found a bug in his coffee. When the waiter returned the cup to the table, the diner said it was the same coffee. How did he know?

2. I take up no space yet can fill up an entire room. What am I?

3. I go up and down yet never move. What am I?

4. You are running in a competition and pass the person in second place. What position would you be in?

5. Which is correct to say, "The yolk of the egg are white" or "The yolk of the egg is white?"

6. What is the greatest use of cowhide worldwide?

7. What American State is surrounded by the most water?

8. If you have me and you share me, you no longer have me. What am I?

9. I can be filled with empty hands. What am I?

10. Scratch my head, and I'm now black when once I was red. What am I?

Seek and Find

Dustin, Matthew, Jill, and Katie are cousins. They each vacationed in one of the following states: Mississippi, Ohio, New York and Washington. Their transportation varied as well. It included a motor home, a plane, a car, and a van.

For each cousin, identify the State they visited and transportation, based on the following information.

- The cousin in the car did not drink coke. Matthew drank coke. The cousin in the plane had a coke with Katie.
- Jill visited the Empire State Building.
- Dustin said, "Buy new rims for your van, Jill. I saw some during my trip to Mississippi."
- The cousin in the plane mentioned that he had seen corn fields in Ohio.

Cousin	State	Transportation
Matthew	__________	___________
Katie	__________	___________
Dustin	__________	___________
Jill	__________	___________

Celestial Directions

Complete the puzzle so that the required numbers and symbols are used only once in every 3-by-3 box, every row, and every column: 1 2 3 ○ ☆ ↑ ↓ ☽ ☾

			↑		☽	☾		
			☆	↓			☽	
☆			○				1	
	↑				2		○	☾
		○				☽		
2	☽		1				3	
	3				↓			○
	↓			☾	☆			
		1	3		○			

Secret Codes

Fill in the blanks

A-26, F-21, K-15,

R ___, ___ X

Divide

64 ÷ 8 =	30 ÷ 6 =	32 ÷ 4 =
24 ÷ 3 =	30 ÷ 3 =	36 ÷ 6 =
21 ÷ 7 =	30 ÷ 10 =	70 ÷ 10 =
32 ÷ 8 =	21 ÷ 3 =	48 ÷ 8 =
8 ÷ 1 =	9 ÷ 3 =	35 ÷ 5 =
5 ÷ 5 =	27 ÷ 3 =	10 ÷ 2 =
7 ÷ 1 =	36 ÷ 9 =	45 ÷ 5 =
40 ÷ 4 =	24 ÷ 4 =	81 ÷ 9 =
20 ÷ 4 =	24 ÷ 6 =	54 ÷ 9 =

Completion Times: ______,

_______, _______, _______, ________

A Card for All Seasons

How many cards and how many differences does your brain perceive?

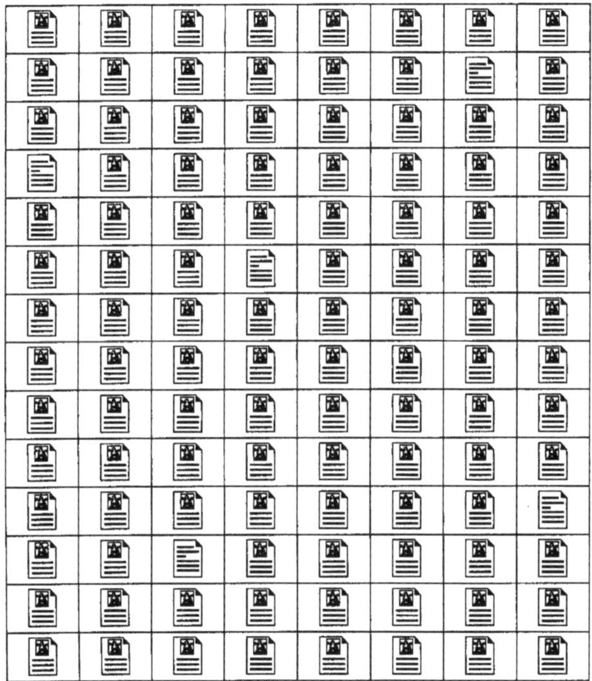

True or False – Brain Wiring

Axons form the largest projection from neurons and are the brain's equivalent of electrical wires. They are each only about one one-hundredth of the thickness of a human hair in diameter.

Brain Tip

Avoid brain dehydration by making certain you drink plenty of pure water on a daily basis

Brain Bits

Both the brain and the body require a consistent supply of pure water. The body is composed of about 70% water, give or take a few percentage points. The brain is composed of closer to 80% water.

Chronic dehydration is believed to be a major but preventable contributor to premature aging. Estimates are that the majority of people over the age of 50 are dehydrated, especially if their practice is to drink water based on perceived thirst.

Dehydration contributes to an increase of free radicals within the body. Free radicals are behind all manner of problems from forming wrinkles on your skin to actually destroying brain cells.

Strive for bodily cleanliness, as well. Regular bathing helps to remove impurities from your skin and can reduce the likelihood of their being reabsorbed.

According to a report attributed to the Mayo Clinic, healthy adults should drink one milliliter of water for every calorie burned.

Chapter Fifteen

A Drop in a Bucket…

Memory and imagination are twins. Memory is the historical diary of where you have been; imagination is the creative map of where you are headed.
—Arlene Taylor

It may take longer for an older brain to arrive at solutions for a specific problem, but the solutions may be of higher quality on average than those from younger brains. Creative activities can help the brain remain flexible.

For example, take the old axiom, "He who laughs last laughs best." Ask your brain to come up with alternative endings. Here are some examples:

He who laughs last…

- …isn't paying attention
- …is trying to be polite
- …just doesn't get it
- …has molasses for brains
- …is laughing to fit in or may be clueless
- …may be practicing inadvisable restraint
- …is trying to decide if anything was funny
- …is behind the times
- …doesn't want a repeat performance

Refer to *Double Dog Dare* in Chapter 11 - Make a Long Story Short.

Complete each of the statements in that chapter by adding one or more alternative endings. Make them as innovative as you wish—whatever makes sense to your brain.

Get together with family and friends and share your alternative endings. Brainstorm more endings. It's worth the effort to your brain, and you will likely have a great deal of fun in the process!

Did You Know?

When you recall familiar information, and couple that with viewing the information in a new way, your brain can really get some exercise. Writing and solving riddle-type puzzles can help your brain with this type of thinking. Take this one for example:

"I can pass directly in front of the sun without making a shadow. What am I?"

Your brain has stored information about the sun and shadows. Sort through that stored information.
As your brain keeps recalling and creatively sorting the information, it may come up with the words "wind" or "air." Suddenly a possible solution clicks into place. Of course! Wind or air can pass directly in front of the sun without making a shadow.

X Marks the Spot

How many X's and how many differences
does your brain perceive?

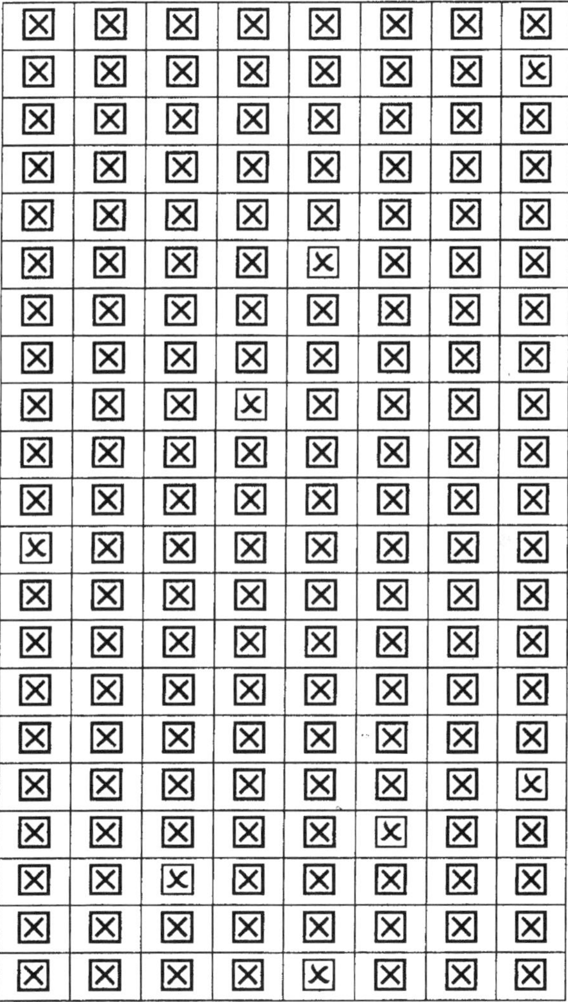

What Did You Just Say?

Solve the following riddles.

1. I am as light as a feather. You can hold me but usually for only a minute or two. What am I?

2. I run but do not walk. I have a mouth but you won't find me talking. I have a head but weep not, and while I have a bed I never sleep. What am I?

3. Forward, you need heavy equipment to move me, but backward I am not. What am I?

4. Wherever you may roam you can find me right in the middle of nowhere. What am I?

5. I am the best and the worst thing in the world. What am I?

6. The more of me you take, the more of me you leave behind. What am I?

7. I can go up a drain pipe down but I cannot go down a drain pipe up. What am I?

8. What is the invention that got things rolling?

9. You can see straight through me, and I'm so fast you can't see me. I don't stop until the day you die. What am I?

Did You Know?

Most loss of mental capacity happens to the very old and is related more to lack of exercise, drug interactions, depression, or other reversible conditions than to simply the process of aging.

Unmask the Mask

What does your brain perceive?

True or False – Brain Play

Studies have shown that adults who regularly stimulated their brains (e.g., reading, playing chess or bridge, listening to music) were two to five times less likely to develop Alzheimer's disease.

Target Practice

How many targets and how many differences does your brain perceive?

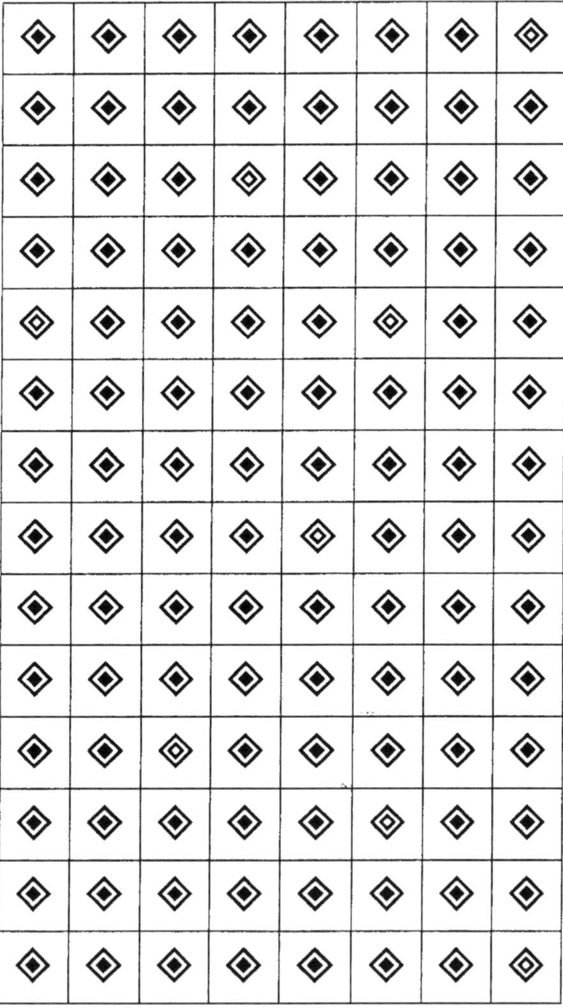

More Bolts from the Blue

Solve the following riddles.

1. I am served at a table in gatherings of two or four. Small, white, and round, you need me to have fun, and that's part of the fun. What am I?

2. I can spare eight, lest I lose my one. I'm not a number. What am I?

3. I die until you call me again. Each time you call, you hear from me. What am I?

4. The dirtier I am, the whiter I get. What am I?

5. I have no beginning, end, or middle. Many people consider me a delicacy. What am I?

6. I have skin and more eyes than one. I am very nice when I am done. What am I?

7. I am as big and deep as a cup, but even a river can't fill me up. What am I?

8. How many times can you subtract the number 5 from 25?

9. I come in many shapes and sizes. You likely have at least one of me, and my history you tell. What am I?

10. I am harder to catch the faster you run. What am I?

Around the World

How many worlds and how many differences does your brain perceive?

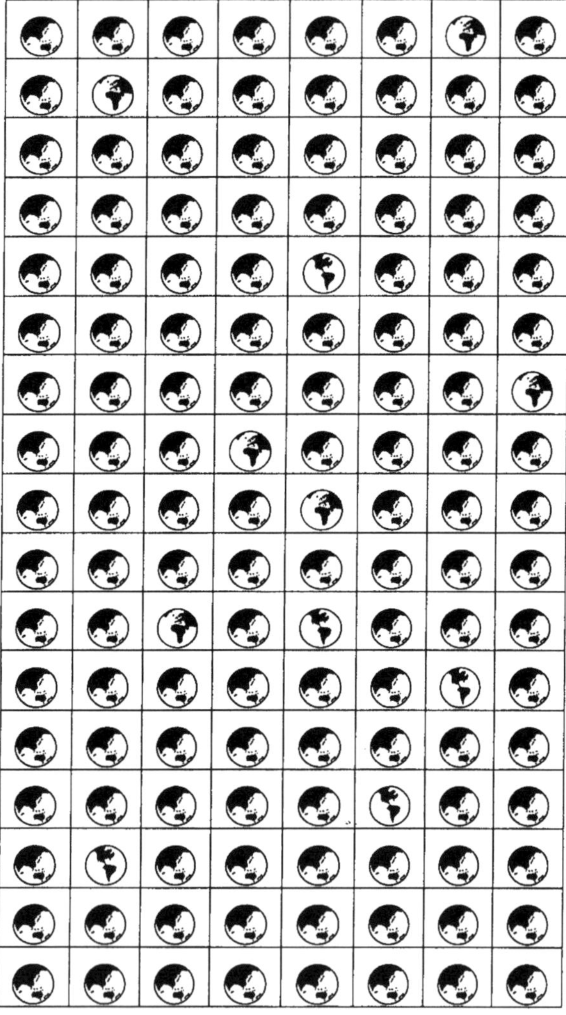

Thinking Smarter Not Harder

Solve the following riddles.

1. If an orange house is made from orange clay and a red house is made from red clay and a gray house is made from gray clay and a black house is made from black clay, what is a greenhouse made from?

2. The pink house is one story and absolutely everything in it is pink. The doors are pink, the sofa is pink, and the refrigerator is pink. What color are the stairs?

3. Who kept house for Sherlock Holmes?

4. Say "silk" five times. Now spell "silk." What do cows drink?

5. To prepare me, you throw away the outside and cook the inside. When you eat me, you eat the outside and throw away the inside. What am I?

Did You Know?

About half of people learn best when they approach a new subject "top down" (start with a broad view).

The other half do best when they analyze it "bottom up" (begin with the facts).

All the World's a Stage

Complete the puzzle so that the required letters are used only once in every 3-by-3 box, every row, and every column: MIND STAGE

M			A	S	T			E
			M		N			
		N		G		M		
N	M	T				S	E	I
	A		S	N	I		T	
S	G	I				A	D	N
		D		A		E		
			D		E			
E			I	M	G			D

Did You Know?

Playing a musical instrument can give the brain a good workout and can be an excellent form of challenging mental stimulation.

Brain Benders 15-1

1.	2.
READ LEBAL	**MAINTENANCE**

3.	4.
1 1 1 1 1 1 **LIGHTLY**	**HE** **GNIRAEB**

5.	6.
TIDAH U	**S U F F E** **R I N G**

7.	8.
APPRECIATED **EHS**	**NERVE**

9.	10.
TI FRACS	**chicken**

Brain Tip

Build opportunities into your schedule for fun and relaxation

Brain Bits

According to Michael F. Roizen, MD, author of *Real Age,* there is a relationship between stress and aging. The faster you rev your body with stress, the more quickly you age. Physically, chronic stress alters immune responses.

All work and no play makes for deadly, dull, and dreary living. Sometimes a change can be as good as a rest. In fact, the brain thrives on variety. Fun and relaxation can be good stress reducers.

Many individuals stay so busy with personal and professional activities that they rarely take time to laugh, play, and have fun.

Laugh while you exercise and play. Laugh while you work and learn. Laughter stimulates the production of endorphins, which have been found to strengthen the body's immune system.

To paraphrase Mary Poppins: a day full of laughter makes the medicine go down!

Chapter Sixteen

The More the Merrier…

Be not afraid of growing slow;
be afraid only of standing still.
—Chinese Proverb

Solving Brain Benders can help to stimulate your creativity. Don't think you're creative? Studies have shown that the single common denominator among people judged to be creative was that they *believed* they were creative!

You can improve your own creativity by believing you are creative and by taking full advantage of your own brain's unique abilities.

The same thought processes used to solve problems can also generate creative ideas (e.g., finding new connections, making new associations, and thinking outside the box).

Thinking creatively can mean looking at things in a new way. For example, winners tend to picture themselves as winning.

Creativity thrives in an atmosphere of encouragement but shrivels in the presence of fault finding and criticism. Deliberately surround your brain with positive, happy, and affirming people.

Brain Benders 16-1

1.	2.
I I T I I	**K C A B**
3.	**4.**
PLAYALP	**UPIT**
5.	**6.**
BLAC TAOC	**MINEM U**
7.	**8.**
END DNE	**YELL**
9.	**10.**
R E D R O	**T O U C H**

The Winner Is

Which one does your brain think is most accurate?

1. Three coins in a fountain, each one selling happiness.
2. Three coins in a fountain, each one is seeking happiness.
3. Three coins in a fountain, each one seeking happiness.
4. Three gold coins on a mountain, each one filled with happiness.

Circles Make Squares

What does your brain perceive?

True or False – Rehearsal

Visualization is often utilized by athletes in their training (e.g., repeatedly picturing an ideal performance). When they actually perform, their minds and bodies tend to follow these pre-established configurations.

Brain Benders 16-2

1.	2.
HEAD NOISILLOC	**EARTH 🡅**

3.	4.
SYMPHON	**DAYOR**

5.	6.
CYCLE CYCLE CYCLE	**PARK**

7.	8.
D O W N	**E C ECNALG A L G**

9.	10.
STAR	**WEAT HER**

Prime Calculations

Complete the puzzle so that the required numbers and symbols are used only once in every 3-by-3 box, every row, and column: + 1 – 3 × 5 ÷ 7 =

		×						+
		=	3			÷	5	–
		–	1	÷				
		+					=	1
			+		=			
=	5					×		
				5	–	7		
×	3	7			÷	+		
–						1		

Did You Know?

Unconscious memories can impact your in-the-moment perception, which in turn can impact your body's biochemistry and hormone production.

The Human Mind

Solve for the phrase by Oliver Wendell Holmes

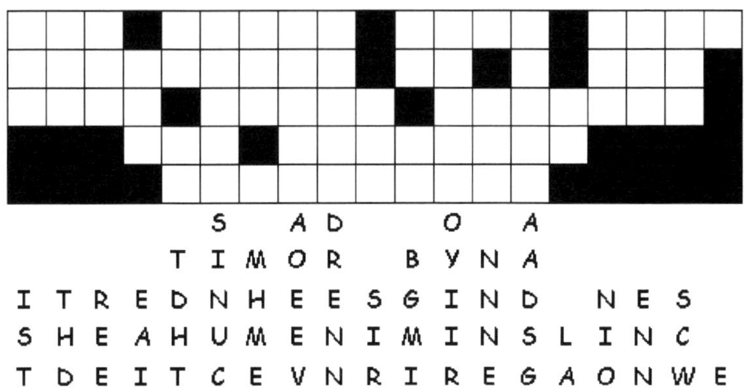

Boxes ’N Boxes

What does your brain perceive?

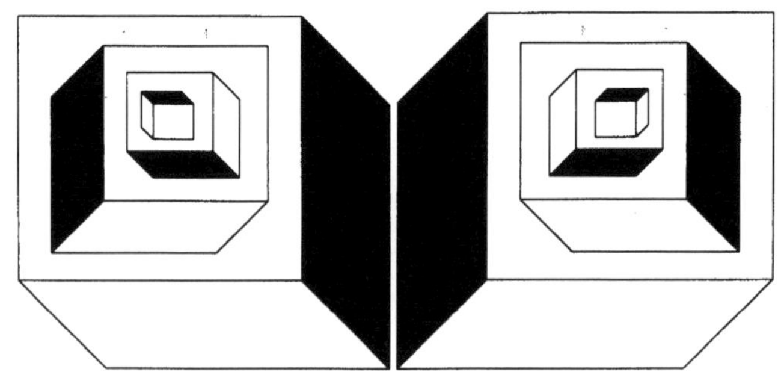

Playing Around

Complete the puzzle so that the require letters are used only once in every 3-by-3 box, every row, and every column: MIND PLAYS

I			P		L			Y
D			Y		A			S
L	A						D	
	Y			S			I	
S		P	A		N	Y		D
	D		L	P			S	
	S						Y	I
Y			D		P			M
	M			Y	S		P	

Did You know?

Visualizing (internal mental picturing) can help improve performance for musicians and athletes. PET scans showed that brain areas involved in imagining (e.g., complex or skilled movements) surround the areas that are activated when the movements are actually made.

Brain Benders 16-3

1.	2.
FOURUOF	**HOMUDSE**

3.	4.
GRAPH HPARG GRAPH HPARG GRAPH	**UP UP UP UP UP UP UP**

5.	6.
D E R	**D N U O R A**

7.	8.
ESUOH PRAIRIE	**GIGIGIGI CCCCCCCC**

9.	10.
_ HOPPIN _	**REMMAH TAT TAT**

African Safari

The game preserve is packed with hunters. Seventeen of them are on a huge safari motor-caravan. One hunter lost an arm during military service and thirteen wear glasses.

Each has an identical backpack containing a baker's dozen clothing items, including hats, gloves, boots, and scarves for each. How many hands are in the caravan, and how many gloves are in the packs?

Looking Over a 4-Leaf Clover

What does your brain perceive?

True or False – Clowning Around

Laughter stimulates both sides of the brain and actually enhances learning. It eases muscle tension and psychological stress, which helps to keep the brain alert and promotes retention of information.

Left, Right, Left

How many figures and how many differences does your brain perceive?

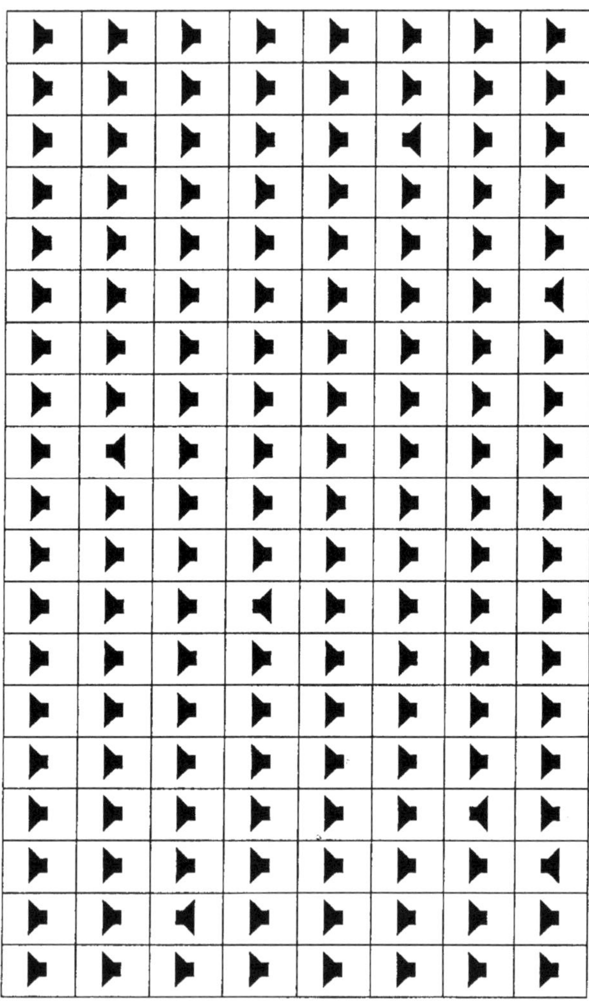

Did You Know?

Studies by Dr. Lee Berk of Loma Linda University have shown that increases in Beta-Endorphins and Human Growth Hormone are associated with the anticipation of laughter, as well as with the actual experience of laughing.

Slinking Along

Where does your brain perceive the opening to be on each figure?

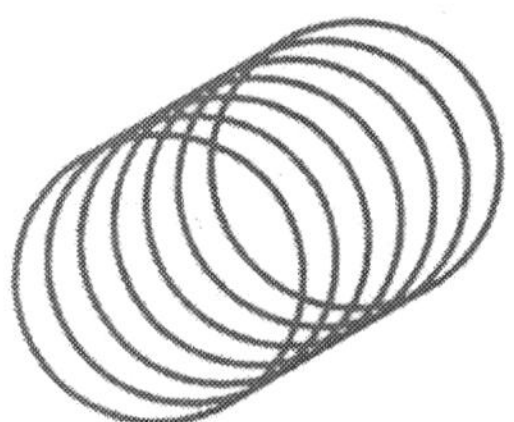

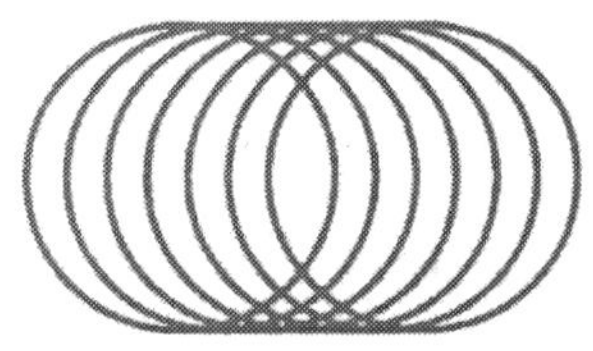

True or False – Energy

Positive thoughts and feelings add energy to your system and are “energy assets.”

Negative thoughts and feelings (e.g., anxiety and anger) deplete your store of energy and are “energy eaters.”

Brain Tip

Believe your brain is creative—it is

Brain Bits

Everything begins in your brain. In order to achieve anything, you must first believe in yourself and your creative ability.

Think of creativity as holding an idea up to the light, much as you would a multifaceted diamond. As you slowly turn the diamond, the light strikes it in different ways, allowing you to see different facets.

Creativity is a way of seeing things not perceived before. It can involve a new idea, a new bridge between existing ideas, or a combination of both.

Einstein reportedly developed some of his best creative ideas when doing other things such as walking, holding a conversation, or daydreaming (e.g., imagining what it might be like to ride on a beam of light and look back at a clock).

Many tend to think of creativity primarily in relation to artistic endeavors. It is, however, a key ingredient of effective problem-solving. Thank your brain for helping you be more creative in a variety of different ways. It is only too willing to help.

Chapter Seventeen

From Here to Kalamazoo...

Whether you believe you can do something or you believe you can't, you're right.
—Old Proverb

The brain needs a constant supply of blood in order to keep up with the heavy metabolic demands of the neurons.

Approximately 20% of the blood flowing from the heart is pumped to the brain, although the brain accounts for only 2% of the mass of your entire body.

The brain does not have much room to store nutrients, however, as space is limited by the skull. According to Neil Nedley, MD, the frontal lobes require blood flow with a steady and adequate glucose level in order to achieve peak performance.

When neural activity is stimulated, your brain gobbles up glucose from your bloodstream. If your brain is short on fuel, it cannot function efficiently.

Brain-imaging techniques such as functional Magnetic Resonance Imaging (fMRI) rely on this relationship between neural activity and blood flow to produce images of reduced brain activity.

Brain Benders 17-1

1.	2.
U P S I D E	**C A CARPETCARPETCA P E T**
3.	**4.**
DATOHSRK	**NOIS ICED**
5.	**6.**
H E A D S	**Y R R U H**
7.	**8.**
YLTHGILS CAST	**NEVER YADNUS**
9.	**10.**
STREERTEET	**WODEYDOL**

Clear as a Bell

The letters in the words of these common sayings are scrambled (the word order is not), and the last word is missing. Decipher the scrambled saying and select the missing word from the answer options.

For example: etrtbe tale nath____.

❑ story	❑ never
❑ snake	❑ always

The answer: *better late than never*

1. eh acn't ese the rtsefo orf eht …

❑ honesty	❑ trees
❑ promise	❑ face

2. eh sha a lwoloh...

❑ arm	❑ leg
❑ shoulder	❑ mouth

3. solok gdoo eughno ot...

❑ drink	❑ wonder
❑ eat	❑ beast

4. dam sa na dol tew...

❑ hen	❑ frog
❑ bird	❑ snake

5. eth yelar drib tseg hte...

- ❑ radish
- ❑ sunlight
- ❑ garden
- ❑ worm

6. kame yah lehiw eht nsu...

- ❑ drops
- ❑ rains
- ❑ shines
- ❑ clouds

7. o'ndt yrc rveo pitls...

- ❑ water
- ❑ present
- ❑ earned
- ❑ milk

8. kyemon ese, nmoeyk...

- ❑ broth
- ❑ do
- ❑ get
- ❑ wish

9. tac tog uyro...?

- ❑ answer
- ❑ slip
- ❑ dog
- ❑ tongue

10. kpase ltoysf dna rayrc a gib...

- ❑ stick
- ❑ ball
- ❑ present
- ❑ honesty

Wine, Women, and…

What does your brain see first?

Did You Know?

Challenging mental exercise can alter the shape of a dendrite in 30 seconds and grow a new one in 30 minutes.

This appears to be especially helpful for the prefrontal lobes and the hippocampus—areas of the brain that are involved with memory, recall, and cognition.

Back in the Good Ol' Days

Answer the following questions.

1. A rectangular cherry cobbler has a single rectangular slice missing, and you want to divide what's left equally between you and a friend with a single straight cut. How should you do this?

2. You are in a room where the walls, ceiling, and floor are six feet thick. There are no doors, windows, or other openings. The only items that are in the room with you are a mirror and a table. How do you get out?

Note: This is a riddle to which there is no *logical solution*!

3. You are given a five-quart jug and a three-quart jug. You are sent to a lake and told to come back with exactly one gallon of water. How do you come up with exactly one gallon of water?

4. A race car driver went three blocks the wrong way down a one-way street without breaking the law. How can this be?

5. What are the next 2 letters of this sequence

A E F H I K L M?

6. Why can't you take a picture of a shepherd with sheep?

7. Why are 1999 dollars worth more than 1998 dollars?

8. What is unique about the number 859172?

9. How can you throw a ball and make it stop and come back to you without it touching anything or having anything attached to it?

10. A man drove all the way across the United States without knowing he had a flat tire. Explain.

11. A child trotted all the way across a lake without sinking into the lake. How did he do this?

12. Lillian's mother, Mrs. Jensen, had only four children. The oldest, a boy, she named North. The next oldest, a girl, she named South. The third, a boy, she named East. The youngest child was another girl. What was her name?

Brain Benders 17-2

1.	2.
O U T	**TIMING: ON** **<u>OFF</u>**

3.	4.
√C√H√I√N√E√S√E√	**ONE $ $ $ $**

5.	6.
TOWORHTEL	**TUNNELTHGIL**

7.	8.
SIGN – – – – – – –	**<u>SIT</u>** —— ——

9.	10.
TWO FUNNY **YNNUF OWT**	**STRYLAP EET**

Five Flakes in a Fountain

How many flakes and how many differences does your brain perceive?

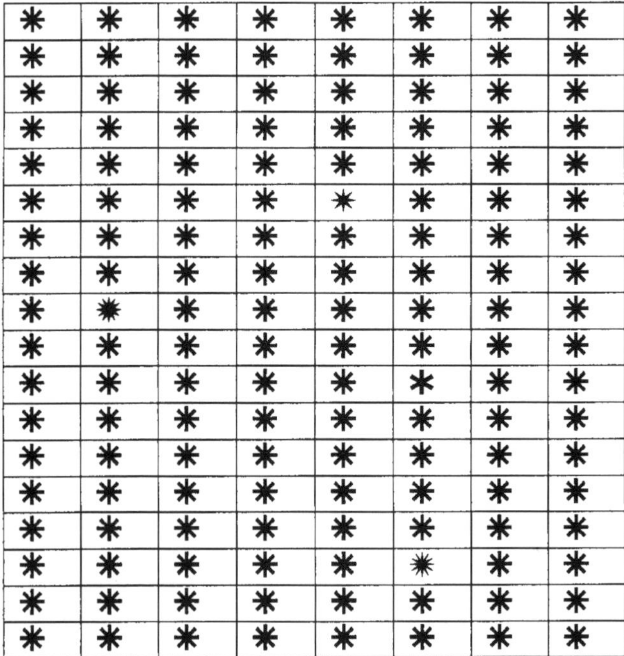

True or False – Workplace

Studies have shown that employees who laugh together "stay together." They tend to work better as a team, are more creative, and produce more work.

Finishing up

1. List ten, three-letter words for body parts.

2. Add to a baker's dozen the number of Boeing's 747 Superjet, baseball's *stretch* inning, the number saved by a stitch in time, and what a golfer yells before hitting a long shot.

Subtract the total number of blackbirds baked in a pie and the number of miles driven in the Indianapolis Memorial Day Race.

Divide by the number of birds in the hand that one in the bush is worth. Answer?

3. Matthew went out to buy some baseball equipment. He spent half of what he had plus $5 at the first store. He spent half of what was left plus $4 at the second store. At the third store he spent half of the remainder plus $3. He then had $5 left to buy base balls. How much money did he start with?

4. Dustin, Christy, Jill, Katie and Aimi took a physic's exam. Aimi was not last. Katie was not first or last. Aimi scored higher than Christy, Katie higher than Jill, and Dustin lower than Christy but higher than Katie. Who had the highest score?

Brain Benders 17-3

1.	2.
DISPLAY	**TRAFKCUTSFIC**
3.	**4.**
SINGING **YEK**	**DEKRAM**
5.	**6.**
N O O **O KCEN S** **O S E**	**PROELASGRESS**
7.	**8.**
ECON **OM** **IC**	**GNIKLAW** **GGE SHELLS**
9.	**10.**
RAKED **SLAOC**	**DEPPORD**

Brain Tip

Honor, appreciate, and enjoy the complexity of your brain

Brain Bits

Development of the human brain continues throughout life. Learning forges new connections in the neural network at every age.

Every thought you think is believed to actually change the structure of your brain.

The bad news for couch potatoes is that more than their muscles are at risk for getting soft and flabby. The brain can deteriorate, as well.

If you stop learning, your overall performance and mental capacity will decline due to a weakening and eventual loss of brain networks—neural connections.

You may find that some behaviors are easy to learn and to do. Others may be easy to learn and hard to do. Some are hard to learn and hard to do.

When something is easy to do and you hardly remember learning to do it, that's called talent.

Chapter Eighteen

Wrap Your Brain Around It...

Old age must be resisted and its deficiencies supplied.
—Cicero

Your own biology is controlled by what you believe. Belief is the "eye" of your spirit, according to noted cardiologist Arnold Fox, MD. What you believe in does influence what you get.

If you see health, happiness, and success, your spirit will respond to that vision by setting in motion various biochemical events that can lead to increased health, productivity, and energy.

You are composed of many energy systems that encompass thoughts, feelings, and emotions. Every thought can be energetically calibrated for its impact on your body and your environment.

You choose the thoughts you think about, and you think about what you believe. Your behaviors follow your beliefs. To alter your behaviors you must change your thoughts.

Believe that the steps you are taking toward age-proofing your memory will help to strengthen your intelligent/creative memory.

Brain Benders 18-1

1.	2.
TOTEGUCH	**RAB**
3.	**4.**
EMIT **8**	**MOULDING** **FLEHS**
5.	**6.**
FALLINGPEELS **PEELS**	**GOING** **POT**
7.	**8.**
HSIW **STAR**	**APUIR**
9.	**10.**
DIGESDABTION	**TOO YNNUF** **FUNNY TWO**

Up and Down

How many arrows and how many differences does your brain perceive?

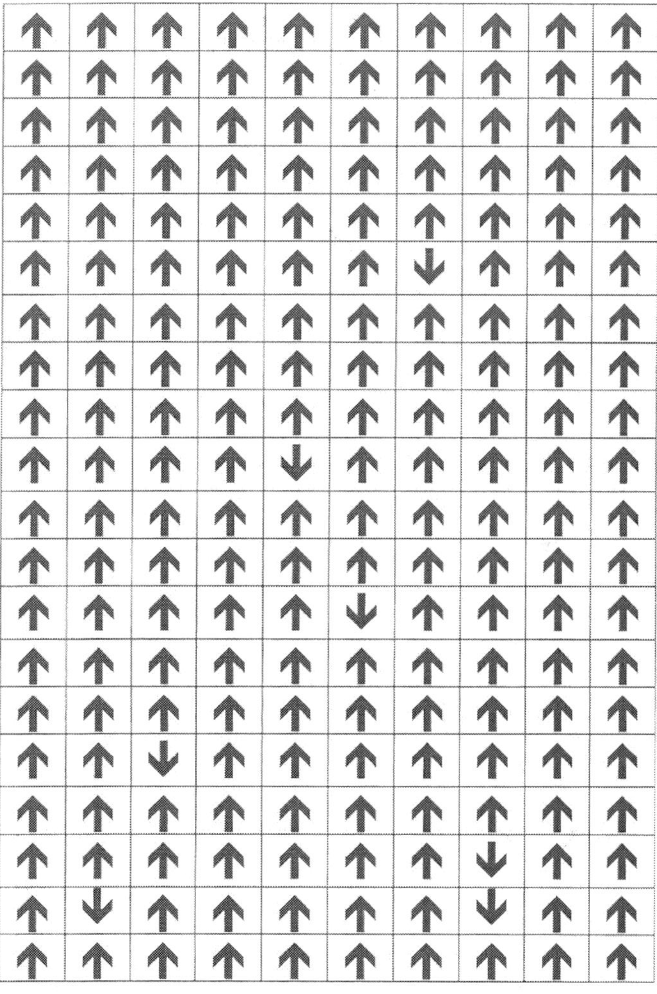

Hup Two XYZ

Complete the puzzle so that the required letters and faces are used only once in every 3-by-3 box, every row, and every column: ☺ 😐 ☹ **T W O X Y Z**

		😐			**X**		**Y**	**T**
Y						**Z**	**O**	
	O				**W**			☹
X			**T**	☹				
	W						**T**	
				Y	**Z**			😐
☺			😐				**Z**	
	😐	**T**						☺
	Y		☺			**O**		

Did You Know?

Spirituality, although difficult to describe, tends to utilize functions of the right hemisphere, as compared with *proclamation* that tends to utilize left-hemisphere functions.

Brain Benders 18-2

1.	2.
⎕ ← GNIKOOL	CHECKOUTCHECKOUT

3.	4.
TROHS PATIENCE	NEWS

5.	6.
TRAFFICTRAFFIC	TITNEMOME

7.	8.
AR SET EST TER IN	PPP AAA RRR KKK I I I GNN GGG

9.	10.
LIPS SPIL	UNLIKELY

Calculate Calculate

5 x 6 =	6 – 2 =	1 x 9 =	3 x 2 =
16 ÷ 4 =	6 + 9 =	5 x 5 =	3 + 5 =
6 + 8 =	0 + 6 =	9 ÷ 3 =	8 ÷ 4 =
9 x 9 =	7 x 3 =	14 – 9 =	7 x 4 =
7 x 1 =	8 – 1 =	6 ÷ 3 =	4 + 9 =
1 x 1 =	1 x 5 =	9 x 5 =	13 – 8 =
4 + 9 =	4 + 0 =	20 ÷ 2 =	10 – 7 =
15 – 6 =	15 – 6 =	13 – 4 =	15 – 8 =
2 x 5 =	2 + 2 =	5 x 5 =	8 – 3 =
9 – 1 =	10 ÷ 2 =	9 ÷ 3 =	4 + 1 =
10 – 4 =	10 – 2 =	14 – 9 =	1 + 0 =
13 – 6 =	1 x 5 =	6 ÷ 3 =	14 – 7 =
5 x 5 =	8 x 2 =	9 x 5 =	8 ÷ 4 =
9 ÷3 =	18 ÷3 =	3 x 5 =	3 + 7 =
10 – 9 =	3 x 1 =	1 x 8 =	3 + 3 =
9 + 5 =	7 + 7 =	7 – 4 =	12 ÷ 2 =
10 – 6 =	9 x 6 =	10 ÷ 5 =	0 x 7 =
9 + 1 =	9 x 6 =	7 x 7 =	4 x 3 =

Completion Times: _______,

_______, _______, _______, ________

Diamond Doings

How many diamonds and how many differences does your brain perceive?

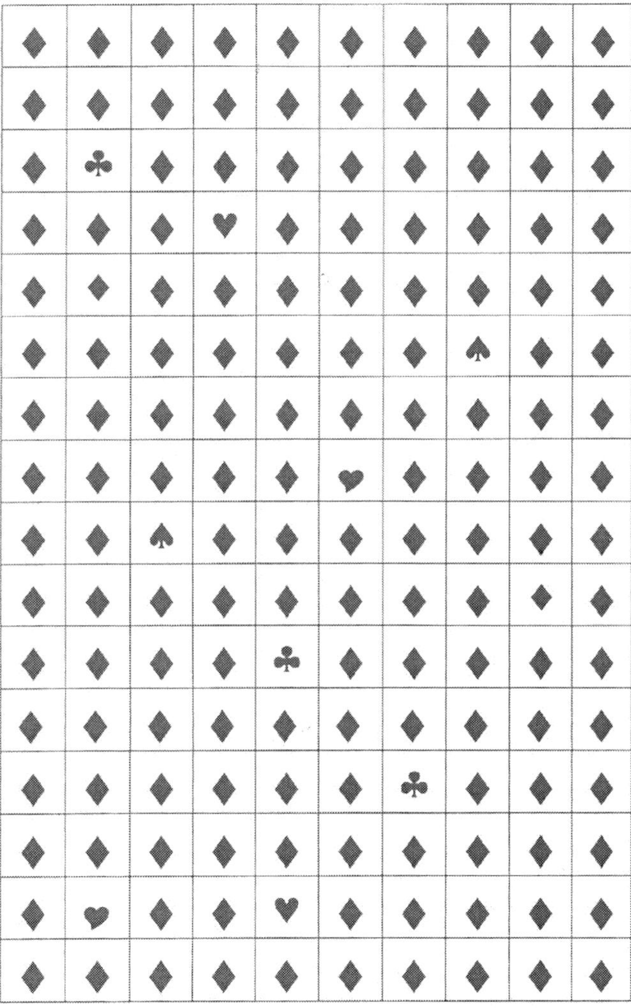

Barking up the Wrong Tree

Answer the following questions.

1. What is full of holes but can still hold water?

2. What has no content yet you can see it?

3. What falls but never breaks?

4. What is it that goes with an automobile, is of no use to it, and yet the automobile cannot move without it?

5. An interesting statistic shows that more Chinese males eat rice than Japanese males. What is the reason?

6. There is a barrel with no lid and some cider in it. Robert thinks it is more than half full while Alice thinks it is less than half full. Without measuring implements or removing any cider from the barrel, how can they easily determine who is correct?

7. Three switches outside a windowless room are connected to three hot plates inside the room. How can you determine which switch is connected to which hot plate if you are only allowed to enter the room once?

Did You Know?

When you picture a desired outcome, you give your brain a map to follow. Without a defined target, the mind's energy is squandered.

Mirror, Mirror on the Wall…

Whose pillars are thickest overall?

True or False – Bundles

Large bundles of nerve fibers form bridges that connect the two hemispheres of the human brain. Three important groups of commissural tracts are the:

- Corpus callosum
- Anterior commisure
- Posterior commisure

Recalculate

11 – 7 =	1 x 9 =	3 x 5 =	9 ÷ 3 =
10 – 9 =	6 + 2 =	1 x 8 =	14 – 9 =
2 + 1 =	6 + 9 =	7 – 4 =	6 ÷ 3 =
9 + 2 =	0 + 6 =	10 ÷ 5 =	9 x 5 =
8 x 9 =	7 x 3 =	7 x 7 =	20 ÷ 2 =
6 + 6 =	5 + 6 =	12 – 3 =	13 – 4 =
11 – 7 =	1 x 9 =	3 x 5 =	9 ÷ 3 =
3 – 1 =	5 x 6 =	8 – 1 =	3 + 5 =
6 x 7 =	16 ÷ 4 =	1 x 5 =	8 ÷ 4 =
1 + 1 =	6 + 8 =	4 + 0 =	7 x 4 =
3 x 8 =	9 x 9 =	15 – 6 =	4 + 9 =
18 ÷ 3 =	7 x 1 =	2 + 2 =	13 – 8 =
6 x 7 =	1 x 1 =	10 ÷ 2 =	10 – 7 =
11 – 3 =	4 + 9 =	10 – 2 =	15 – 8 =
8 + 4 =	13 – 6 =	7 + 7 =	15 – 9 =
5 + 5 =	5 x 5 =	9 x 6 =	15 ÷ 5 =
5 + 3 =	9 ÷3 =	6 x 9 =	4 ÷ 2 =
3 x 3 =	10 – 9 =	12 – 6 =	16 – 2 =

Completion Times: ______,

_______, _______, _______, ________

True or False – Back and Forth

There are asymmetries between the two hemispheres and, to some degree, they orchestrate differing functions.

For example, Broca's area (audible speech) and Wernicke's area (heard speech) are both in the left hemisphere.

Walleyed

What does your brain perceive?
Does the position of the figure make a difference?

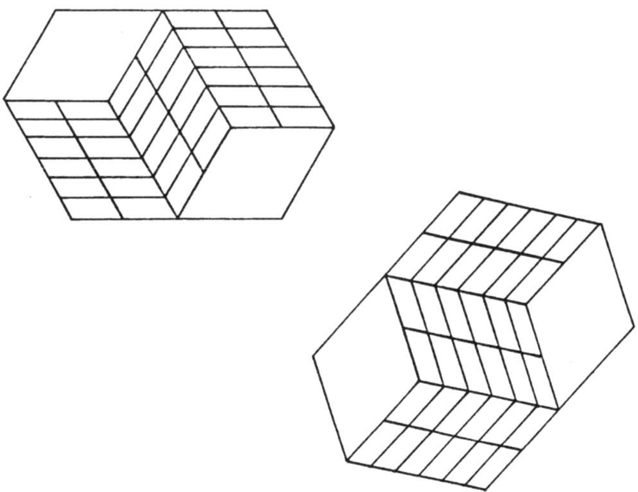

Brain Tip

Exercise your brain's memory mechanisms on a daily basis

Brain Bits

Develop a whole-brained approach to strengthening your memory and recall abilities. Engage in multiple strategies rather than concentrating on just one.

Memories form when a pattern is repeated frequently or under circumstances that encourage the pattern to be encoded. Each time a group of neurons fire together, the tendency to do so again is increased.

Unless you take steps to transfer information from short-term into long-term memory and then rehearse recall, about 60% of all you learn is forgotten within an hour—80% within one month! For some brains, saying information aloud can help transfer it into long-term memory more easily.

Unfortunately, the failure to actively flex your memory "muscles" can result in atrophy.

Preventing memory loss will always be easier than restoring it. The best protection is to exercise the brain's memory mechanisms on a daily basis.

Chapter Nineteen

The Sky's the Limit…

The tragedy of life is not that it ends so soon but that we wait so long to begin it.
—W. M .Lewis

Congratulations!

You've reached the end of *Age-Proofing Your Memory!*

Go through the book several more times. Each time your brain will likely solve the exercises more quickly and easily.

Create, share, or exchange puzzles with others who are interested in how to *die young at a very old age,* as the old saying goes.

Surround yourself with friends who have a positive mindset and who are having fun with the aging process.

Creatively expose your brain to variety and to something new every day.

You only have one brain with which to remember, and only you can take care of it! The sky is the limit when it comes to your intelligent/creative memory.

Brain Tip

Consider taking a nutritional product designed to support brain function

Brain Bits

Some have said that you change the cells in your body every six or seven years—except for your neurons. You basically have what you have. Invest the time to learn how to care for your brain and its neurons.

In the book *Discovered: Nature's Secret Fountains of Youth, A Report from the American Commission on Anti-Aging,* Robert Concoby, C.N.C. wrote:

"Today it is possible to live longer…affordable anti-aging basics are available for anyone."

Key micronutrients have been identified to help to support brain and immune system function. These include C-Q10, L-theanine, enzymes, and green superfoods.

Every positive step you take toward strengthening your brain and age-proofing your memory can pay you exponential dividends.

Start now—the brain you save may be your own!

Brain Tips

Making a List 'n Checking it Twice…

For some brains *out of sight is out of mind.* To make it easy for those brains to review Brain Tips, here they are in the order in which they appear in this book.

Hang out with smart people and be proactive in challenging your memory on a daily basis.

Read aloud for at least ten minutes a day

Develop personal life satisfaction based on what is important to you and your brain

Increase your personal knowledge about the aging process and take conscious steps to retard the onset of aging symptoms

Do yourself and the world a favor and become now the person you want to be when you are older

Live a high-level wellness lifestyle and take personal responsibility for factors within your partial or complete control

Develop a positive mindset and cultivate a happy face—it's an instant face-lift

Exercise daily to keep your brain and body in the best possible condition

Anticipate retaining your memory and affirm daily that you are recalling needed information in a timely manner

Eat nutritious meals at regular times, using foods that are in as natural a state as possible

Make caring for your brain part of your daily routine

Create and maintain realistic expectations

When you are unable to avoid a negative stressor, apply the 20:80 Rule

Take responsibility for getting the optimum amount of sleep your brain needs

Avoid undesirable brain dehydration by making certain you drink plenty of pure water on a daily basis

Build opportunities into your schedule for fun and relaxation

Believe your brain is creative—it is

Honor, appreciate, and enjoy the complexity of your brain

Exercise your brain's memory mechanisms on a daily basis

Consider taking a nutritional product designed to support brain function

Solutions – Last Resort…

People don't grow old.
When they stop growing they become old.
—Sanford Graves

You will likely realize the most benefit if you come up with your own answers before you review the ones that follow.

Be persistent. Keep trying to solve the brain aerobic exercises, even if you keep coming back to one of them for several days.

Once you have solved a specific brain aerobic exercise, try your hand at crafting a similar exercise to share with your friends. This can further help to stimulate your intelligent/creative memory.

Remember that the single most common characteristic of people deemed to be creative was that they believed they were!

Chapter Two – Time's Awasting

The Eyes Have it: Your brain may perceive the short line moving toward the front, or the openings of the two boxes changing. The eyes usually appear to remain on the back side of each box.

Double Header

Set #1: 187, 188, 189; 763, 764, 765

Set #2: 16, 37, 79, 142, 262

Nothing like Flying: Your brain may perceive four boxes or four partial rooms. Looking one way it may appear as if the goose is escaping from the box. Viewed another it may appear as if the dove is flying into the box.

Start to Finish

1. 20, 24
2. N – Nine
3. 24, 96
4. S – Saturday
5. 24, 12
6. J – July
7. 5 40
8. C – Christmas, or X for X-mas
9. E – Eighty (10, 20, 30 …)
10. S – Seventh (1st, 2nd, 3rd …)
11. N – Nine (1, 2, 3 …)
12. M – Letters on a keyboard
13. 125
14. 2123
15. J for July (Jul through Dec backwards)

Flocking Together: Your brain may perceive a goose or dove flying depending on which side of the page your eyes view first. A person's "lead eye" may look at the opposite side of the page first. Your brain may find it easier to perceive the outlined figures or the solid figures.

Yee-Haw: This figure represents a series of numbers (1-5) each with its mirror image beside it.

Money Matters

?	%	#	7	$	8	9	&	!
&	7	!	%	?	9	$	#	8
9	$	8	#	&	!	?	7	%
%	!	?	$	9	&	7	8	#
#	8	7	?	!	%	&	$	9
$	&	9	8	#	7	!	%	?
7	9	%	!	8	$	#	?	&
8	#	&	9	7	?	%	!	$
!	?	$	&	%	#	8	9	7

Would You Believe it?

1. Same
2. Stamp collector
3. Earth atmosphere
4. Australia
5. John Adams

Odd Signs

9	1	○	5	◇	□	3	7	△
◇	5	3	△	7	9	○	1	□
7	□	△	1	3	○	◇	5	9
○	9	7	□	△	1	5	3	◇
3	◇	5	9	○	7	△	□	1
1	△	□	3	5	◇	9	○	7
5	3	9	7	1	△	□	◇	○
□	7	◇	○	9	5	1	△	3
△	○	1	◇	□	3	7	9	5

True or False – Half and Half: True

Stars Get in Your Eyes: 7 different figures and at least 16 differences overall.

Brain Benders 2-1

1. Not up to par
2. Splitting hairs
3. Block head, square head
4. Move up or move down
5. Tennis
6. High fives, high seas
7. Splitting headache
8. Sit on it
9. Stick it in your ear
10. One after another

Negotiations Heading South: Does your brain perceive the goblets first or the profiles in the stems? Can you imagine what the conversation was about and reasons that it went awry?

Balancing Act: Your brain may perceive two blocks connected by interlockings.

Chapter 3 – Use It or Lose It

Brain Benders 3-1

1. Brain bender
2. Eggs over easy
3. Somewhere over the rainbow
4. Once upon a time
5. Looking back
6. You're under arrest
7. Tool box
8. Swimming around
9. In the heat of the battle
10. Water (H_2O) "The letter H to the letter O"

Change in the Weather: 6 Differences

Brain Benders 3-2

1. Scrambled eggs
2. In and out
3. Left over lunch
4. An inside job
5. What's up
6. Feedback
7. Right over wrong
8. Rock around the clock
9. Read between the lines
10. Time is on my side

Two Times Two

I	N	F	O	D	S	U	M	R
U	O	R	M	I	N	D	F	S
M	S	D	F	U	R	I	N	O
S	F	N	U	O	I	R	D	M
O	D	I	R	M	F	S	U	N
R	U	M	S	N	D	F	O	I
D	R	O	N	S	U	M	I	F
F	M	U	I	R	O	N	S	D
N	I	S	D	F	M	O	R	U

True or False – Vividly: False. The brain finds it difficult to perceive the difference between something you vividly imagine and something you actually experience.

Famous Lines: All the world's a stage and all the men and women merely players (William Shakespeare).

The Winner Is: Your brain may perceive two boxes with a "winner" on the end of each or two partial rooms with a "winner" painted on two of the walls. Your brain may even perceive a large black book in the center pointing toward or away from you.

In Your Cups: Observe the cups and the facial profiles in each stem. Two people meet, start talking, and then laugh. Create a scenario about what triggered their laughter.

A Fine Kettle of Fish

1. Towel
2. Onion
3. Twenty-third
4. 364
5. Leaves
6. Radishes (they have to be dug out of the ground)

7. A potato

Hearts are Bustin' out All over: 5 differences

Between You and Me: Me, you, coy. What else does your brain perceive?

True or False – Really? True, according to Richard Restak, MD, in *Mozart's Brain and the Fighter Pilot.*

Take Care of Your Heart: Some think the first figure resembles two pairs of lips shaping a heart. There are no diamonds – just white spaces. Your brain will likely find the heart in the gift box obvious. There is no "X" – just white spaces.

True or False – Ages: True

Flower Fantasia: 112 flowers with at least 5 differences

Chapter 4 – Lend Me an Ear

Musical Metronome

2	🕒	U	4	C	1	T	N	O
O	1	T	2	🕒	N	C	4	U
N	4	C	U	T	O	1	2	🕒
1	T	4	N	O	2	🕒	U	C
🕒	C	O	T	4	U	N	1	2
U	2	N	C	1	🕒	4	O	T
C	N	1	O	U	T	2	🕒	4
4	U	🕒	1	2	C	O	T	N
T	O	2	🕒	N	4	U	C	1

True or False – Slowing: False. Slow music and music in minor keys tend to stimulate alertness in the brain's cortical and limbic areas.

Brain Benders 4-1

1. Short on rations
2. Take in a movie
3. Bridge to nowhere
4. Drive along the coast
5. Running on fumes
6. Broken pencil
7. Dead end
8. Insider trading
9. Get on board
10. Dry up, high and dry

Music Recall: Do this exercise with friends. Help each other recall. It can be fun in a group.

The Notes Have it: 9 Differences

Brain Benders 4-2

1. You're too good to be true
2. Back stab
3. Routine check up
4. Clean up
5. Arrive on time
6. Bowling on the green
7. A pain in the tail
8. Kick high, kick up
9. End of the decade
10. Flashback

Musical Challenge

4	🕛	5	🔔	♈	2	♫	3	1
🔔	♫	1	3	🕛	4	2	5	♈
2	♈	3	1	5	♫	🕛	4	🔔
5	1	♫	🕛	2	3	🔔	♈	4
♈	2	4	♫	🔔	5	3	1	🕛
3	🔔	🕛	4	1	♈	5	2	♫
1	3	2	♈	♫	🕛	4	🔔	5
🕛	5	🔔	2	4	1	♈	♫	3
♫	4	♈	5	3	🔔	1	🕛	2

True or False – Tandem: True

Brain Benders 4-3

1. You're under arrest
2. Flash in the pan
3. Pain in the neck
4. Bats in the belfry
5. Up in the clouds
6. Up to bat
7. Frame it
8. She's beside herself
9. Growing smaller
10. For pity sake

Do You Hear What I Hear? 8 Differences

Chapter 5 – As Smart as a Steel Trap

Half Moon Rising: 9 differences

Right Left, Left Right: The words appear to be facing toward the right or left or back and forth, depending on your own brain.

Square Off: Minimum of 5

Toot Your Own Horn:

> **Months with 30 days:** All but February. Mnemonics hint: 30 days hath September, April, June, and November. All the rest have 31 save February alone. Leap year coming once in four, February then has one day more.
>
> **Colors in a rainbow:** Red, orange, yellow, green, blue, indigo, and violet. Mnemonics hint: Richard Of York Gave Battle In Vain.

The Same and Different: Each represents a piece of equipment made by humans and each represents a way in which to communicate with others.

Square Has It: Minimum of 14

Five American Great Lakes

- Lake Huron—third-largest by volume and second-largest in area
- Lake Ontario—second-smallest in volume, smallest in area, much lower elevation
- Lake Michigan—second-largest by volume, third-largest by area; only one entirely in the U.S.
- Lake Erie—smallest by volume, shallowest
- Lake Superior—largest by volume, area, and depth

Possible Uses for an Orange

1. Make orange juice
2. Peal and eat
3. Dice for a Jell-O salad
4. Throw as a ball
5. Use as a candle-stick holder
6. Scoop out for a toy boat
7. Paper weight
8. Candy the rind for fruit cake
9. Represent the earth in a solar-system model
10. Add sections to a green salad

Squared Again: Minimum of 25

True or False – Einstein: True

Square Wares: Minimum of 88

Times Square: Minimum of 66

Peaks, Peaks, and More Peaks

1. The big island of Hawaii
2. Mt. Everest
3. Black Hills
4. Cascade Range
5. Mt. McKinley or Denali
6. Mt. Fuji
7. Matterhorn in the European Alps

Brain Benders 5-1

1. Out house
2. Canine
3. Upside down
4. Misunderstand
5. The center of attention
6. Small worries
7. Mind's eye

8. Eating on the run
9. Middle of the week
10. Lone wolf

Capitals of the 50 US States and D of C

Alabama, Montgomery
Alaska - Juneau
Arizona - Phoenix
Arkansas - Little Rock
California - Sacramento
Colorado - Denver
Connecticut - Hartford
Delaware - Dover
District of Columbia - Washington
Florida - Tallahassee
Georgia - Atlanta
Hawaii - Honolulu
Idaho - Boise
Illinois - Springfield
Indiana - Indianapolis
Iowa - Des Moines
Kansas - Topeka
Kentucky - Frankfort
Louisiana - Baton Rouge
Maine - Augusta
Maryland - Annapolis
Massachusetts - Boston
Michigan - Lansing
Minnesota - St. Paul
Mississippi – Jackson
Missouri - Jefferson City
Montana - Helena
Nebraska - Lincoln
Nevada - Carson City
New Hampshire - Concord
New Jersey - Trenton
New Mexico - Santa Fe
New York - Albany
North Carolina - Raleigh
North Dakota - Bismarck
Ohio - Columbus
Oklahoma - Oklahoma City
Oregon - Salem
Pennsylvania - Harrisburg
Rhode Island - Providence
South Carolina - Columbia
South Dakota - Pierre
Tennessee - Nashville
Texas - Austin
Utah - Salt Lake City
Vermont - Montpelier
Virginia – Richmond
Washington – Olympia
West Virginia - Charleston
Wisconsin -Madison
Wyoming - Cheyenne

And the Location is…Oops: Depending on your brain the bust may be facing a wall or mounted on top of a pillar, or may appear to move back and forth.

True or False – Neuroscience: True

Chapter 6 – A Sense in Time Saves Mine

Stars, Stars, and More Stars

1. Oprah Winfrey
2. Charlie Gibson
3. Robin Roberts
4. Ellen Degeneres
5. Larry King
6. John McCain
7. Barrac Obama
8. Hillary Clinton
9. Pope Benedict XVI
10. Reverend Billy Graham
11. Angelina Joli
12. Harrison Ford
13. Michael Phelps

When it Strikes, it Strikes: Your brain may perceive streaks of lightening but this is only due to spaces between the dark portions of each figure.

Divide:

72 ÷ 8 = 9	12 ÷ 6 = 2	4 ÷ 4 = 1
27 ÷ 3 = 9	15 ÷ 3 = 5	60 ÷ 6 = 10
28 ÷ 7 = 4	10 ÷ 10 = 1	60 ÷ 10 = 6
49 ÷ 7 = 7	3 ÷ 3 = 1	32 ÷ 8 = 4
9 ÷ 1 = 9	6 ÷ 3 = 3	25 ÷ 5 = 5
20 ÷ 5 = 4	21 ÷ 3 = 7	2 ÷ 2 = 1
8 ÷ 4 = 2	4 ÷ 1 = 4	12 ÷ 4 = 3
27 ÷ 9 = 3	50 ÷ 5 = 5	33 ÷ 11 = 3
6 ÷ 2 = 3	64 ÷ 8 = 8	30 ÷ 5 = 6

Match the Sport – Recall

1. Hockey
2. Baseball
3. Golf
4. Basketball

5. Football
6. Ice Skating and Dancing with the Stars

True or False – Sleep: True

Brain Benders 6-1

1. A fish out of water
2. Line up
3. Riding in the rodeo
4. Mesmerized by her
5. Paper trail
6. Running in place
7. Ball is in your court
8. Look behind you
9. Jumping up and down
10. The top 50

I Beg Your Pardon: 7 Differences

Strike While the Iron is Hot

1. Cubic centimeter, liter
2. Gram, ounce
3. Yard, mile
4. Centimeter, meter
5. Blocks, kilometer
6. Inches, foot
7. Feet, yard
8. Feet, mile
9. Eight
10. 12 dozen or 144
11. Eight
12. Ounces, gallon
13. 2.5
14. Pounds
15. Kilometer
16. Quarts
17. Gallons
18. 160
19. Circle, 3.14

Brain Benders 6-2

1. A small world after all
2. Media bias
3. Mixed company
4. Too hot to handle
5. Adverse
6. Big trouble
7. Incomplete recovery
8. Wrong, doesn't add up
9. Misunderstand
10. Humpty-Dumpty took a great fall

True or False - Heredity: False. For most people, lifestyle choices and behaviors have a greater impact.

Stairs and Towers: Your brain may perceive stairs or walls or towers changing position. Does the position of the figure make a difference? Close your eyes for a moment and when you open them the figure should be in its original position.

Brain Benders 6-3

1. Peaceful in death
2. Drive at the speed limit
3. Working on a deadline
4. Too late at night
5. Open for dinner
6. Worried over nothing
7. Humpback whales
8. Hiding around the corner
9. Look both ways
10. Workers on strike

Chapter 7 – Got My Mojo On

Subtract

7 -3 4	4 -4 0	10 -5 5
7 -2 5	10 - 2 8	9 -3 6
9 -8 1	8 -4 4	7 -6 1
7 -7 0	9 -2 7	6 -5 1
4 -1 3	8 -4 4	8 -1 7
5 -4 1	8 -2 6	9 -1 8
15 - 4 9	18 - 2 16	17 - 6 11

A New Wrinkle in My Old Horn

1. A nickel and a half dollar. Only one is not a half dollar.
2. Seven
3. The sun is shining; there's no rain.
4. Short
5. There isn't any smoke. It's an electric train.
6. All of them

7. They were two of triplets.
8. The only place each window could have a southern exposure is on the north pole. So the bear must have been a polar bear. The answer, therefore, is white.
9. He's born in room number 1975 of a hospital and dies in room number 1995.
10. Post Office
11. Eight thousand. When books sit on shelves, the first page of the book is the rightmost page, and the last page is the leftmost page. So you can't count the pages in the first and last volumes.
12. Dead
13. A mirror
14. A glove
15. Soul

Spring and Fall: Your brain may perceive a beautiful young woman and an ancient crone. It may identify these easier depending on the way in which the image faces as compared to your lead eye.

Outside the Box

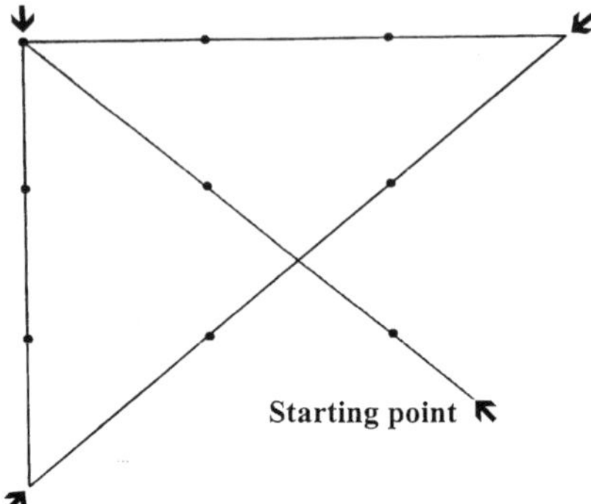

Between You, Me, and the Fence Post

1. He is the preacher
2. The island is a traffic island
3. Bruce is a horse
4. It's a model train set
5. Thursday is a horse
6. He was a skywriter whose plane crashed into a student's plane
7. Stove, fire, smoke
8. Nineteen
9. 182
10. A coffin
11. A tissue
12. All states
13. He was lying (no coins were dated prior to Christ's birth because the birth had not yet occurred)
14. You are the driver. How old are you?
15. Playing different people
16. One, each one after that is an anniversary
17. A dozen apples (or 27 cherries)
18. You can't bury someone alive
19. Six
20. He at a hotel and is unable to sleep -the man in the adjacent room is snoring. He phones the snorer who wakes up and answers. The first man hangs

up without saying anything and goes to sleep before the snorer begins snoring again.

21. He is a mail courier who delivers packages to foreign embassies in the United States. The land on which the embassy stands belongs to the country of the embassy, not to the U.S.

True or False – Lifestyle: True

Brain Benders 7-1

1. Riding low; low riding
2. Crying Shame
3. Tax on tea
4. Four square
5. Mixing it up
6. Annual check up
7. Face up to it
8. Get over it
9. Jumping through hoops
10. Gossip Column

Proverbial Puzzles

1. A bad hair day
2. A day late and a dollar short
3. A diamond in the rough
4. A face only a mother could love
5. Make hay while the sun shines
6. A fate worse than death
7. A fool and his money is soon parted
8. A friend in need is a friend indeed
9. Legend in his own time
10. A man's got to do what a man's got to do
11. A penny for your thought
12. Get while the getting's good

True or False – Education: True

Hands and More Hands: 8 different shapes, 14 differences

Chapter 8 – Keep Your Eyes Peeled

Book Worms: Your brain may perceive it pointing away from you, or toward you, or both.

True or False - Enculturation: True

Brain Benders 8-1

1. Sitting bull
2. All around town
3. South pole
4. 12th of Never
5. Walleyed
6. Split infinitive
7. Six feet under ground
8. Pie in the sky
9. Middle of nowhere
10. Middle of the day

Can't Take my Eyes off of You: The openings will likely change depending on how long your look at each figure.

True or False – Sensibility: True. More seems to be understood about vision than about some of the other senses.

True or False – Mmm-m-m-m: False. Actually the reverse is true. The retina in the male brain typically contains more "M" cells, designed to detect motion. The retina of the female brain typically contains more "P" cells, designed to detect color and texture.

Eye Opening: Some brains find it easier to locate openings when the box contains a dot.

Brain Benders 8-2

1. Tea for two and two for tea
2. Split atoms
3. See-through blouse
4. Never ending change, continual change
5. Cubic zirconia
6. Box car
7. Tacky
8. Hairs standing on end
9. Head over heels in love
10. Time on my hands

Cubic Synfonia: A minimum of 13 cubes in each figure

Daffynitions

1. Cesarean Section	A district in Rome
2. Outpatient	Person who has fainted
3. Organic	One who works on organs
4. Protein	One who likes young people
5. Serology	English knighthood study
6. Paralyze	A couple of untruths
7. Nitrate	Lower than the day rate
8. Morbid	A higher offer
9. Diagnostic	Die not believing in a deity
10. Adenoid	Bothered by commercials
11. Medical staff	A doctor's walking stick
12. Artery	Study of fine paintings
13. Stalemate	An old spouse or partner
14. Eyedropper	A clumsy ophthalmologist
15. Dilate	To live longer
16. Barium	When CPR fails
17. GI series	Games between soldiers
18. Hangnail	A coat hook
19. Postoperative	A letter carrier
20. Vein	Inflated opinion of oneself
21. Intravenous	A goddess enters
22. Colic	Lassie
23. Avoidable	What bullfighters do

24.	Intense	Where campers sleep
25.	Eclipse	Gardener does to hedge
26.	Coffee	Break fluid
27.	Belong	To take up your time
28.	Rubberneck	To help a friend relax
29.	Coma	A punctuation mark
30.	Congenital	Very friendly

Proof, Proof, What a Goof: 12 "F" or "f" letters

True or False – On Board: True

Chapter 9 – A Diamond Is Forever

Diamonds and More: 12 differences

Brain Benders 9-1

1. West side story, story line, side story, tall story
2. Scabs
3. Open after hours
4. Toy gun, son of a gun
5. Stop on a dime
6. Double or nothing
7. Broken speech
8. I overate
9. Tit for tat
10. Love letter

Exercise Equipment

M	B	Y	S	R	A	I	G	N
S	R	A	I	N	G	Y	M	B
I	N	G	B	Y	M	S	R	A
N	Y	B	G	M	S	R	A	I
R	A	S	N	B	I	M	Y	G
G	M	I	R	A	Y	N	B	S
B	S	M	A	I	R	G	N	Y
Y	I	N	M	G	B	A	S	R
A	G	R	Y	S	N	B	I	M

Shorthand Sequences:

A-1, D-4, H-8, L-12, P-16, T-20 (every 4th letter and number beginning with A=1 and increasing toward Z)

I Knew That!

1. Smiles (a mile between the first and last letter)
2. An ax-i-dent
3. A cheetah
4. Armed
5. 116 years (1337-1456)
6. Honduras
7. A pet degree
8. Tennis (played with a racket)

All in a Whirl: Your brain will likely perceive that the circles are drawn in a way that could not happen in real life.

True False – All Heart: False. The brain needs 20-30 times more blood than other body organs. Poor posture reduces blood flow in two main arteries that pass through the spine to the brain hindering thinking, mental performance, and other cognitive functions. Sit up straight (Maggie Greenwood-Robinson PhD, in *20 / 20 Thinking*).

Brain Benders 9-2

1. Foreign affairs
2. Fancy
3. Writer's block
4. Bottom of the barrel
5. Potatoes (spuds) by the pound
6. Blue in the face
7. The Big apple
8. Fifty-one
9. Multiple, or too many expectations
10. Personal loan (lone N)

It's Time: 4 differences

Four and Seven Make Eleven:

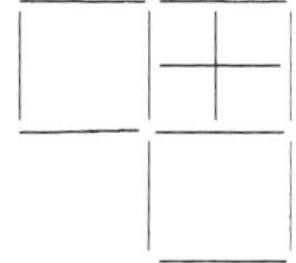

Merry-Go-Round:

All letters above the line have angles;
all letters below the line have curves

Bolts from the Blue

1. A stamp
2. A hole
3. Time
4. Fire
5. Nothing
6. A cloud
7. Wholesome
8. A heart
9. The letter "e"

It's in the Directions: 8 differences

True or False – Lost: True

Help Us All

1. A cold or the flu
2. A fire
3. Elephant's shadow
4. One degree
5. Bread
6. You're name, you're driving
7. Neither: each is on a island in a river
8. A library, it has the most stories

Chapter 10 – Time to Bite the Bullet

Text Messages

®	1	Ⓟ	©	5	4	⊗	3	2
⊗	5	3	®	2	Ⓟ	©	4	1
©	2	4	1	⊗	3	Ⓟ	®	5
5	®	⊗	Ⓟ	1	©	4	2	3
4	3	1	⊗	®	2	5	Ⓟ	©
2	Ⓟ	©	3	4	5	1	⊗	®
Ⓟ	⊗	2	5	©	®	3	1	4
1	4	5	2	3	⊗	®	©	Ⓟ
3	©	®	4	Ⓟ	1	2	5	⊗

True False – Nimble Thimble: True

You've Got to be Joking

1. One minds the train, the other trains the mind
2. A-sharp major
3. A tow truck
4. A sculptor (always chiseling), or a con artist
5. A Voltswagen
6. A toothless squirrel
7. A southpaw
8. Doesn't matter what you call it, it can't come
9. Hush puppies
10. One baits his hooks, the other hates his books
11. One minds his peas, the other minds his cues
12. A jeweler sells watches; a jailer watches cells

Arrows and More

9	3	←	7	↑	→	5	↓	1
↑	↓	5	←	9	1	→	3	7
7	→	1	5	3	↓	←	9	↑
↓	5	3	↑	1	7	9	→	←
1	↑	→	9	←	3	↓	7	5
←	7	9	↓	→	5	1	↑	3
5	1	↓	3	7	9	↑	←	→
3	9	↑	→	5	←	7	1	↓
→	←	7	1	↓	↑	3	5	9

True False – Yours or Mine: True

Multiply

6 x3 18	2 x2 4	10 x8 80
7 x3 21	10 x6 60	9 x5 45
9 x6 54	8 x3 24	7 x4 28
7 x5 35	9 x7 63	6 x6 36
9 x4 36	8 x7 56	7 x6 42

7	9	6
x3	x9	x4
21	81	24
9	9	9
x3	x7	x4
27	63	36

Ring Around the Rosy: 15 differences

Double Dog Dare

1. Earned
2. Heart
3. Nine
4. Learn
5. Money
6. Texas
7. Bird
8. Knowledge
9. Reckoning
10. Sucker
11. Snails
12. Dirt
13. Brick
14. Foot, grave
15. Pudding
16. Sock
17. Scalded
18. Stone
19. Wit
20. Banshee
21. Skill, luck
22. Snot
23. Turnip
24. Shadow
25. Night, day
26. Link
27. Fuel
28. Twig, tree
29. Well, well
30. Mind, gutter
31. Load or deck
32. Fate
33. Bird, two in the bush
34. Words
35. Words
36. Madness
37. Bun
38. Feather
39. Done
40. Arm, leg
41. Fancy
42. Leg
43. Grasshopper
44. Toes

It's More than Water

N	S	V	M	W	E	I	D	A
M	D	E	S	I	A	W	N	V
W	I	A	V	N	D	E	S	M
D	M	S	N	E	I	A	V	W
A	N	I	D	V	W	S	M	E
V	E	W	A	S	M	D	I	N
E	W	M	I	D	V	N	A	S
S	A	D	W	M	N	V	E	I
I	V	N	E	A	S	M	W	D

Squares and More Squares: 168

Brain Benders 10-1

1. Mirrors in the room
2. Clock on the wall
3. Ninety
4. Book on the shelf
5. Long underwear
6. You are overextended
7. Lost in thought
8. One foot in the grave
9. Mid-morning
10. Cold shoulder

True or False – Altogether now: True according to Jean Marie Stine in the book *Double Your Brain Power*.

Chapter 11 – Make a Short Story Long

Math is Bustin' Out: Except for the "minus" sign, what the brain perceives as mathematical symbols are just impressions based on the way the black squares, lines, and triangles are arranged.

Which Way Out: Your brain may preceive a frantic stick figure on the end of a box inside a box or painted on the wall of a room.

One Plus One

W	N	I	O	B	R	A	S	T
R	S	A	T	N	W	I	O	B
T	O	B	I	A	S	W	N	R
I	R	W	N	T	O	B	A	S
S	B	N	W	R	A	T	I	O
O	A	T	B	S	I	R	W	N
N	I	S	R	W	B	O	T	A
B	T	O	A	I	N	S	R	W
A	W	R	S	O	T	N	B	I

True False – AM or PM: True

It's Miscellani

⊕	☒	2	☑	1	4	5	3	⦸
☑	5	1	3	2	⦸	4	⊕	☒
⦸	3	4	☒	5	⊕	☑	1	2
3	1	⊕	5	⦸	2	☒	4	☑
4	⦸	☑	1	⊕	☒	3	2	5
☒	2	5	4	3	☑	1	⦸	⊕
5	4	⦸	⊕	☑	3	2	☒	1
2	☑	☒	⦸	4	1	⊕	5	3
1	⊕	3	2	☒	5	⦸	☑	4

True False – Banks: False. According to Dr. Candace Pert, former researcher at the National Institutes of Health, memories are stored not only in the brain, but in a psychosomatic network extending into the body.

Brain Benders 11-1

1. Ceiling fan
2. Too hot to handle
3. Up end
4. Running hot and cold
5. Count down to kick off
6. Falling off the roof
7. Bugs in the bed
8. Play in the orchestra
9. She's end over end
10. End of the line

Ain't Just Waltzing Around

1. The letter M
2. When it hugs the shore
3. A dry one
4. Fingers
5. A hole
6. A shoe
7. Silence
8. Glass
9. Echo

Angles and Curves:

- A E, F H, **I** K, L **M**, N **T** (sequential sequences of angular letters)

- B C, D G, J **O**, P Q, **R** S (sequential sequences of rounded letters)

Add

1	8	4
+6	+7	+6
7	15	10
3	6	4
+6	+7	+8
9	13	12
9	8	4
+6	+2	+9
15	10	13
7	9	6
+4	+7	+6
11	16	12
9	8	4
+9	+8	+4
18	16	8

9	12	14
+7	+8	+4
16	20	18
7	9	6
+5	+8	+8
12	17	14

True or False – Memories: True

Brain Benders 11-2

1. Lamp is on
2. Music is too soft
3. Fly on the wall
4. Bird in the hand
5. Backbreaking work
6. Sandwich cut in two
7. Trials and tribulations
8. Engraving on a gold coin
9. Going with you
10. Doctor is out

Chapter 12 – As Luck Would Have It

Happy Days Are Here Again: 144 faces and at least 9 differences.

Odd Suits

♠	3	♥	1	♦	5	7	9	♣
9	♣	7	3	♠	♥	5	♦	1
♦	1	5	♣	9	7	3	♠	♥
1	9	♦	5	3	♣	♥	7	♠
7	♥	♠	9	1	♦	♣	3	5
3	5	♣	7	♥	♠	♦	1	9
♥	7	1	♠	♣	3	9	5	♦
5	♦	9	♥	7	1	♠	♣	3
♣	♠	3	♦	5	9	1	♥	7

It Happened in Scotland: Your two eyes, because you are the person going to St. Ives.

Compound Complexity: Your brain may have a great deal of fun with this composite of several different types of puzzles.

Faces, Faces, and More Faces: This figure came from a 1934 bulletin. Viewed from one direction the man is happy. Turn it upside down and the man is grumpy. Turned on its side your brain may be able to perceive both at once.

True or False – Real Age: False. It is 25 years according to Roizen, Michael F., MD author of *Real Age: Are You As Young As You Can Be?*.

Multiply

1 x 6 6	8 x 7 56	4 x 6 24
3 x 6 18	6 x 7 42	4 x 8 32
9 x 6 54	8 x 2 16	4 x 9 36
7 x 4 28	9 x 7 63	6 x 6 36
4 x 4 16	6 x 9 54	8 x 6 48
6 x 7 42	5 x 4 20	8 x 9 72
3 x12 36	5 x 9 45	7 x 7 49

All Heart

E	T	R	☆	♥	✓	A	🔔	H
H	A	🔔	R	T	E	☆	♥	✓
✓	☆	♥	H	🔔	A	R	T	E
T	H	E	A	☆	R	♥	✓	🔔
A	🔔	✓	♥	E	T	H	R	☆
♥	R	☆	✓	H	🔔	E	A	T
🔔	♥	A	E	✓	H	T	☆	R
☆	E	T	🔔	R	♥	✓	H	A
R	✓	H	T	A	☆	🔔	E	♥

True or False – Funny: False. Studies have shown that males try harder to be funny and are more likely to be trained to be funny. Females may not be trained to be funny. A study involving group therapy sessions showed that men were five times more likely to be funny as compared to women.

Enigma: Bomb cloud, tree, cyclone, face profiles in trunk

Just Checking

1	U	H	✓	E	T	C	O	K
C	T	O	1	K	H	✓	E	U
E	✓	K	U	C	O	T	H	1
T	K	E	H	✓	C	U	1	O
O	1	U	K	T	E	H	✓	C
H	C	✓	O	U	1	K	T	E
U	E	T	C	1	✓	O	K	H
✓	H	C	E	O	K	1	U	T
K	O	1	T	H	U	E	C	✓

True or False – Music: True

Brain Benders 12-1

1. An eye for an eye
2. Hot dog
3. Four seasons
4. The underworld
5. Upward mobility
6. Dial a friend
7. Condescending
8. Banana split, whipped cream on top
9. No end in sight
10. Not quite there

Around the Track

N	O	A	S	G	R	J	B	I
B	S	I	A	J	O	G	N	R
R	G	J	I	N	B	O	S	A
A	B	N	G	I	J	S	R	O
J	R	O	N	B	S	A	I	G
S	I	G	R	O	A	B	J	N
I	A	B	O	S	N	R	G	J
G	J	R	B	A	I	N	O	S
O	N	S	J	R	G	I	A	B

Chapter 13 – Alive and Kicking

One for the Money

6	4	5	1	9	8	2	7	3
1	2	7	3	4	6	5	9	8
8	9	3	2	7	5	4	6	1
5	1	4	6	2	7	3	8	9
2	3	8	4	1	9	6	5	7
7	6	9	8	5	3	1	4	2
4	5	1	7	8	2	9	3	6
9	8	6	5	3	1	7	2	4
3	7	2	9	6	4	8	1	5

Brain Benders 13-1

1. Broke back mountain
2. Whining is increasing
3. Step in a cow pie
4. Soaring above the masses
5. The last song
6. Step in it
7. She's in mourning
8. Dust in your eye
9. Feathers in the wind
10. Fall in a hole

Table Top Plates: Your brain may perceive caricature profiles in the pedestal of the table. Does it make a difference how the pedestal is positioned?

The Hand Has It: #5 may make the most sense to your brain. It would likely depend on the bird as well as a whole host of other factors before you could decide whether it was worth two in the bush. Did your brain pick up the repeated words and did it discriminate among the words "to, too, and two?"

True or False – Couch Potato: False, according to Eric Jensen in *Brain-Based Learning.*

Little Boxes, Little Boxes: Your brain may locate several different opening possibilities.

Traveling Light: 10,990 (7 travelers x 2 = 14 legs. 49 bags x 7 goats = 343. 343 x 7 kids = 2401 343 + 2401 = 2744 x 4 legs = 10,976 plus 14 legs = 10,990)

Two for the Show

7	2	3	9	4	6	8	5	1
5	4	6	2	1	8	3	7	9
9	1	8	5	3	7	4	2	6
1	6	9	4	5	2	7	3	8
2	7	5	6	8	3	1	9	4
3	8	4	1	7	9	2	6	5
4	9	7	3	6	1	5	8	2
6	3	1	8	2	5	9	4	7
8	5	2	7	9	4	6	1	3

North, South, East, West: There are only black triangles and dots in these figures.

Climbing the Walls: Does your brain perceive that the walls change positions?

Add

$\begin{array}{r}1\\+6\\\hline 7\end{array}$	$\begin{array}{r}8\\+7\\\hline 15\end{array}$	$\begin{array}{r}4\\+6\\\hline 10\end{array}$
$\begin{array}{r}3\\+6\\\hline 9\end{array}$	$\begin{array}{r}6\\+7\\\hline 13\end{array}$	$\begin{array}{r}4\\+8\\\hline 12\end{array}$
$\begin{array}{r}9\\+6\\\hline 15\end{array}$	$\begin{array}{r}8\\+2\\\hline 10\end{array}$	$\begin{array}{r}4\\+9\\\hline 13\end{array}$
$\begin{array}{r}7\\+4\\\hline 11\end{array}$	$\begin{array}{r}9\\+7\\\hline 16\end{array}$	$\begin{array}{r}6\\+6\\\hline 12\end{array}$
$\begin{array}{r}4\\+4\\\hline 8\end{array}$	$\begin{array}{r}6\\+9\\\hline 15\end{array}$	$\begin{array}{r}8\\+6\\\hline 14\end{array}$
$\begin{array}{r}6\\+7\\\hline 13\end{array}$	$\begin{array}{r}5\\+4\\\hline 9\end{array}$	$\begin{array}{r}8\\+9\\\hline 17\end{array}$
$\begin{array}{r}2\\+9\\\hline 11\end{array}$	$\begin{array}{r}4\\+7\\\hline 11\end{array}$	$\begin{array}{r}5\\+9\\\hline 14\end{array}$

Three to Get Ready Solution

6	1	5	7	2	4	8	3	9
4	8	7	3	9	5	1	6	2
9	2	3	1	8	6	5	7	4
5	9	8	4	3	2	7	1	6
1	3	6	8	7	9	2	4	5
2	7	4	6	5	1	9	8	3
8	4	9	5	1	3	6	2	7
7	6	2	9	4	8	3	5	1
3	5	1	2	6	7	4	9	8

True or False – Brain Spud: True

Pleasant Potpourri: 152 symbols and at least 50 differences.

Four to Go

9	7	8	2	3	1	5	4	6
3	5	2	4	6	7	9	8	1
4	1	6	9	5	8	3	7	2
8	4	3	5	1	2	7	6	9
5	9	1	7	4	6	2	3	8
2	6	7	3	8	9	4	1	5
1	3	4	8	9	5	6	2	7
7	8	5	6	2	3	1	9	4
6	2	9	1	7	4	8	5	3

True or False – Prevention: False. According to Brent Q. Hafen, et al in *Mind/Body Health,* studies have shown that an optimistic attitude can actually help prevent you from getting sick.

Chapter 14 – More Bang for Your Buck

Brain Benders 14-1

1. Blood on your hands
2. Top banana
3. Side dish
4. Burning the candle at both ends
5. Nurses on strike
6. Weak in the knees
7. Pile of bologna
8. Night is falling
9. Collapse on the bed
10. Morning after the night before

Subtract

$$\begin{array}{r} 6 \\ \underline{-3} \\ 3 \end{array} \qquad \begin{array}{r} 2 \\ \underline{-2} \\ 0 \end{array} \qquad \begin{array}{r} 10 \\ \underline{-8} \\ 2 \end{array}$$

$$\begin{array}{r} 7 \\ \underline{-3} \\ 4 \end{array} \qquad \begin{array}{r} 10 \\ \underline{-6} \\ 4 \end{array} \qquad \begin{array}{r} 9 \\ \underline{-5} \\ 4 \end{array}$$

$$\begin{array}{r} 9 \\ \underline{-6} \\ 3 \end{array} \qquad \begin{array}{r} 8 \\ \underline{-3} \\ 5 \end{array} \qquad \begin{array}{r} 7 \\ \underline{-4} \\ 3 \end{array}$$

$$\begin{array}{r} 7 \\ \underline{-5} \\ 2 \end{array} \qquad \begin{array}{r} 9 \\ \underline{-7} \\ 2 \end{array} \qquad \begin{array}{r} 6 \\ \underline{-6} \\ 0 \end{array}$$

$$\begin{array}{r} 4 \\ \underline{-4} \\ 0 \end{array} \qquad \begin{array}{r} 8 \\ \underline{-5} \\ 3 \end{array} \qquad \begin{array}{r} 8 \\ \underline{-6} \\ 2 \end{array}$$

$$\begin{array}{r} 9 \\ \underline{-4} \\ 5 \end{array} \qquad \begin{array}{r} 8 \\ \underline{-6} \\ 2 \end{array} \qquad \begin{array}{r} 9 \\ \underline{-9} \\ \underline{0} \end{array}$$

12	9	8
-5	-5	-5
7	2	3

It's in the Curls: 9 differences

Upstairs Downstairs: Some brains perceive the stairs turn upside down. If this happens to you, just close your eyes for a moment and when you open them the figure should be in its original position.

Frames Have It: 6 Differences

Think Again Twice

1. He had already put sugar in his coffee
2. Light
3. Stairs
4. Second place
5. Neither. The yolks aren't white.
6. To covers cows
7. Hawaii
8. Secret
9. Glove
10. A match from a book of matches

Seek and Find

Matthew	Ohio	Plane
Katie	Washington	Motor home
Dustin	Mississippi	Car
Jill	New York	Van

Celestial Directions Solution

1	○	↓	↑	2	☽	☾	☆	3
↑	☾	3	☆	↓	1	○	☽	2
☆	2	☽	○	3	☾	↑	1	↓
3	↑	☆	↓	☽	2	1	○	☾
↓	1	○	☾	☆	3	☽	2	↑
2	☽	☾	1	○	↑	↓	3	☆
☽	3	↑	2	1	↓	☆	☾	○
○	↓	2	☽	☾	☆	3	↑	1
☾	☆	1	3	↑	○	2	↓	☽

Secret Codes: A-26, F-21, L-15, R-9, 3-X (every 6th letter and number beginning with A=26 and decreasing toward Z)

A Card for all Seasons: 6 Differences

True or False – Brain Wiring: True

Chapter 15 – A Drop In a Bucket

X Marks the Spot: 168 X's and at least 8 differences.

What Did You Just Say?

1. Your breath
2. A river
3. Ton
4. The letter "H"
5. Nothing
6. Footprints
7. Umbrella
8. The wheel
9. Blink of an eye

Unmask the Mask: Your brain may perceive a pair of aboriginal masks facing each other, or a puff of smoke from a genie's bottle, or …

True or False – Brain Play: True

Target Practice: 112 targets; at least 8 differences

More Bolts from the Blue

1. Ping-pong ball
2. Cat with nine lives
3. An echo
4. Chalkboard
5. Doughnut
6. Potato
7. Kitchen strainer
8. Once only (after that it's no longer 25)
9. Scar
10. Your breath

Around the World: 136 worlds; at least 11 differences.

Thinking Smarter Not Harder

1. Glass
2. Pink
3. None – Holmes was a fictional character
4. Water
5. A cob of corn

All the World's a Stage

M	D	G	A	S	T	N	I	E
A	E	S	M	I	N	D	G	T
I	T	N	E	G	D	M	S	A
N	M	T	G	D	A	S	E	I
D	A	E	S	N	I	G	T	M
S	G	I	T	E	M	A	D	N
T	I	D	N	A	S	E	M	G
G	N	M	D	T	E	I	A	S
E	S	A	I	M	G	T	N	D

Brain Benders 15-1

1. Read the back of the label
2. High maintenance
3. Once over lightly
4. He's overbearing
5. Had it with you
6. Long suffering
7. She is under appreciated
8. Nerve center
9. Scarf it up
10. Chicken Little

Chapter 16 – The More the Merrier

Brain Benders 16-1

1. Exit
2. Back up
3. Play by play
4. Up against it
5. Black overcoat
6. You undermine me
7. End over end
8. Yell down, yellow
9. Order up
10. Touchdown

The Winner Is: The third version is most accurate according to the song made famous by the movie and as sung by Frank Sinatra.

Circles Make Squares: Your brain may perceive a square or a diamond in the center.

True or False – Rehearsal: True

Brain Benders 16-2

1. Head-on collision
2. Middle earth
3. Unfinished symphony
4. Y in the road
5. Tricycle, repeating cycle
6. Central Park, park in the middle
7. Back down
8. Upward glance, backward glance
9. North star
10. Break in the weather

Prime Calculations

5	÷	×	–	=	7	3	1	+
1	7	=	3	+	×	÷	5	–
3	+	–	1	÷	5	=	7	×
÷	×	+	5	7	3	–	=	1
7	–	1	+	×	=	5	÷	3
=	5	3	÷	–	1	×	+	7
+	1	÷	×	5	–	7	3	=
×	3	7	=	1	÷	+	–	5
–	=	5	7	3	+	1	×	÷

All in Your Mind – Solve for the phrase: The human mind once stretched by a new idea never regains its original dimensions (Oliver Wendell Holmes).

Boxes 'N Boxes: Your brain may perceive boxes inside other boxes or walls and floors inside other walls and floors.

Playing Around

I	N	S	P	D	L	M	A	Y
D	P	M	Y	N	A	I	L	S
L	A	Y	S	M	I	N	D	P
A	Y	N	M	S	D	P	I	L
S	L	P	A	I	N	Y	M	D
M	D	I	L	P	Y	A	S	N
P	S	A	N	L	M	D	Y	I
Y	I	L	D	A	P	S	N	M
N	M	D	I	Y	S	L	P	A

Brain Benders 16-3

1. Four by four
2. MD (doctor) in the house
3. Polygraph
4. 7-Up, up up and away, stepping up
5. Red rose, red rising
6. Right around the corner
7. Little house on the prairie
8. Four GI's over seas
9. Shopping center
10. Rat-a-tat-tat

African Safari: 33 gloves in the packs (17 hunters x 2 gloves minus one = 33 gloves, since the hunter with only one arm carries only one glove). There are no hands in the caravan at the moment because they are all ON the caravan.

Looking Over a 4-Leaf Clover: There are only four circles on the page. Due to the more than 90 degree cutouts, however, your brain may think it sees a hexagon.

True or False – Clowning Around: True

Left, Right, Left: 152 figures; at least 7 differences.

Slinking Along: **O**penings moving from one side to the other.

True or False – Energy: True.

Chapter 17 – From Here to Kalamazoo

Brain Benders17-1

1. Upside down
2. Wall-to-wall carpet
3. Shot in the dark
4. Split decisions
5. Heads down
6. Hurry up
7. Slightly overcast
8. Never on Sunday
9. Tree in the Street
10. Dyed in the wool

Clear as a Bell

1. Trees
2. Leg
3. Eat
4. Hen
5. Worm
6. Shines
7. Milk
8. Do
9. Tongue
10. Stick

Wine, Women, and…: If you were using your left hemisphere you might have seen the squarish goblet first; if using the right hemisphere you might have noticed the rounded goblet first. Did you also notice profiles in the stem of each goblet?

Back In the Good Ol' Days

1. Cut the cobbler on a line connecting the center of the cobbler and the center of the missing slice.

2. Look in the mirror. See what you SAW. Use the SAW to cut the table into two halves. Two halves make a WHOLE. Crawl through the WHOLE (hole) to escape.

3. Fill the three-quart jug exactly to the brim and pour it into the empty five-quart vessel. Now refill the three-quart jug and carefully pour as much as will fit into the five-quart jug. Exactly one quart remains in the three-quart jug. Now dump out the larger jug and pour the exact quart into it. Fill the three-quart jug a final time and add it to the quart in the larger container. That makes four quarts—one gallon of water.

4. He was walking

5. N and T. The series consists of characters that are not curved anywhere.

6. Because cameras take pictures, sheep don't.

7. Because 1,999 is more than 1,998!

8. Digits from left to right are arranged alphabetically.

9. You tossed the ball straight up in the air

10. The spare tire was flat

11. The lake was frozen

12. Lillian

Brain Bender 17-2

1. Stretched out
2. Timing is off
3. Chinese checkers
4. One four the money
5. Throw in the towel
6. Light at the end of the tunnel
7. Sign on the dotted line
8. Sit on the side lines
9. Too funny for words
10. Play in the street

Five Flakes in a Fountain: 144 flakes; at least 4 differences.

True or False – Workplace: True

Finishing Up

1. Lip, eye, ear, arm, hip, leg, toe, rib, gum, gut
2. 128
3. $90. ($45. + $5 = $50, $40 left; $20 + $4 = $24, $16 left; $8 + $3 = $11, $5 left).
4. Aimi, Christy, Dustin, Katie, Jill

Brain Benders 17-3

1. Display in the window
2. Stuck in traffic
3. Singing off key
4. Marked up
5. Noose around the neck
6. Sale is in progress
7. Economic downturn
8. Walking on eggshells
9. Raked over the coals
10. Dropped down

Chapter 18 – Wrap Your Brain Around It

Brain Benders 18-1

1. Get in touch
2. Side bar
3. High time, time is up
4. Molding on a shelf
5. Falling to sleep
6. Going over the top
7. Wish upon a star
8. Up in the air
9. Dab of indigestion, bad indigestion
10. Too funny for words

Up and Down: 200 arrows; at least 7 differences.

Hup Two XYZ

W	☹	😐	O	Z	X	☺	Y	T
Y	T	X	☹	😐	☺	Z	O	W
Z	O	☺	Y	T	W	😐	X	☹
X	Z	Y	T	☹	😐	W	☺	O
😐	W	☹	X	☺	O	Y	T	Z
T	☺	O	W	Y	Z	X	☹	😐
☺	X	W	😐	O	☹	T	Z	Y
O	😐	T	Z	X	Y	☹	W	☺
☹	Y	Z	☺	W	T	O	😐	X

Brain Benders 18-2

1. Outside looking in
2. Checkout line
3. Short on patience
4. Great news
5. Bumper to bumper traffic
6. A moment in time

7. Rising interest
8. Parallel parking
9. Tulips, two lips, lips together, fat lips
10. Highly unlikely

Calculate Calculate

5 x 6 = 30	6 – 2 = 4	1 x 9 = 9	3 x 2 = 6
16 ÷ 4 = 4	6 + 9 = 15	5 x 5 = 25	3 + 5 = 8
6 + 8 = 14	0 + 6 = 0	9 ÷ 3 = 3	8 ÷ 4 = 2
9 x 9 = 81	7 x 3 = 21	14 – 9 = 5	7 x 4 = 28
7 x 1 = 8	8 – 1 = 7	6 ÷ 3 = 2	4 + 9 = 13
1 x 1 = 1	1 x 5 = 5	9 x 5 = 45	13 – 8 = 5
4 + 9 = 13	4 + 0 = 4	20 ÷ 2 = 10	10 – 7 = 3
15 – 6 = 9	15 – 6 = 9	13 – 4 = 9	15 – 8 = 7
2 x 5 = 10	2 + 2 = 4	5 x 5 = 25	8 – 3 = 5
9 – 1 = 8	10 ÷ 2 = 5	9 ÷ 3 = 3	4 + 1 = 5
10 – 4 = 6	10 – 2 = 8	14 – 9 = 5	1 + 0 = 1
13 – 6 = 7	1 x 5 = 5	6 ÷ 3 = 2	14 – 7 = 7
5 x 5 = 25	8 x 2 = 10	9 x 5 = 45	8 ÷ 4 = 2
9 ÷3 = 3	18 ÷3 = 6	3 x 5 = 15	3 + 7 = 10
10 – 9 = 1	3 x 1 = 3	1 x 8 = 8	3 + 3 = 9
9 + 5 = 14	7 + 7 = 14	7 – 4 = 3	12 ÷ 2 = 8
10 – 6 = 4	9 x 6 = 54	10 ÷ 5 = 2	0 x 7 = 0
9 + 1 = 10	9 x 6 = 54	7 x 7 = 49	4 x 3 = 12

Diamond Doings: 160 diamonds; at least 10 differences.

Barking Up the Wrong Tree

1. A sponge
2. A hole
3. Night
4. Noise

5. There are more Chinese than Japanese men

6. By tipping the barrel until the cider reaches the rim. If they can see the bottom of the barrel, it is less than half full of cider.

7. Switch on the first switch, leave it on for a minute and then switch it off. Switch on the second switch and enter the room. The second switch will produce heat to the hot plate. The first switch will then be for the hot plate that is warm. The third switch will be connected to the hot plate that is off and cold.

Mirror, Mirror on the Wall: The dark pillars are the same size as the white pillars. The brain tends to perceive dark as smaller.

True or False – Bundles: True

Recalculate

11 – 7 = 4	1 x 9 = 9	3 x 5 = 15	9 ÷ 3 = 3
10 – 9 = 1	6 + 2 = 8	1 x 8 = 8	14 – 9 = 5
2 + 1 = 3	6 + 9 = 15	7 – 4 = 3	6 ÷ 3 = 2
9 + 2 = 11	0 + 6 = 0	10 ÷ 5 = 2	9 x 5 = 45
8 x 9 = 72	7 x 3 = 21	7 x 7 = 49	20 ÷ 2 = 10
6 + 6 = 12	5 + 6 = 11	12 – 3 = 9	13 – 4 = 9
11 – 7 = 4	1 x 9 = 9	3 x 5 = 15	9 ÷ 3 = 6

3 – 1 = 2	5 x 6 = 30	8 – 1 = 7	3 + 5 = 8
6 x 7 = 42	16 ÷ 4 = 4	1 x 5 = 5	8 ÷ 4 = 2
1 + 1 = 2	6 + 8 = 14	4 + 0 = 4	7 x 4 = 28
3 x 8 = 24	9 x 9 = 81	15 – 6 = 9	4 + 9 = 13
18 ÷ 3 = 6	7 x 1 = 7	2 + 2 = 4	13 – 8 = 5
6 x 7 = 42	1 x 1 = 1	10 ÷ 2 = 5	10 – 7 = 3
11 – 3 = 8	4 + 9 = 13	10 – 2 = 8	15 – 8 = 7
8 + 4 = 12	13 – 6 = 7	7 + 7 = 49	15 – 9 = 6
5 + 5 = 10	5 x 5 = 25	9 x 6 = 54	15 ÷ 5 = 3
5 + 3 = 8	9 ÷3 = 3	6 x 9 = 54	4 ÷ 2 = 2
3 x 3 = 9	10 – 9 = 1	12 – 6 = 6	16 – 2 = 8

True or False – Back and Forth: True

Walleyed: The walls appear to change position for some brains. Close your eyes for a moment and when you reopen them, the figure should be in its original position.

Resources

Access *Care of the Brain* under *Brain Facts/References* on Taylor's site:

www.arlenetaylor.org

For information on DVDs, including the companion DVD entitled *Age-Proofing your Memory,* or nutritional products designed to support the brain and the immune-system, or books by the authors go to

www.ThrivingBrain.com/products or

contact Sharlet Briggs at

sharlet@ThrivingBrain.com or

call 1-800-379-5017

Books and DVDs by Arlene R. Taylor PhD and Sharlet M. Briggs PhD are available through:

www.amazon.com

Fund-Raising Opportunity

We partner with schools, churches, and organizations to provide fund-raising opportunities.

Give others the opportunity to purchase *Age-Proofing Your Memory... Using Scripture*—while you earn money for your school, church, or other organizational branch.

Books are provided in lots of fifty (50).

To arrange for this option contact

Sharlet Briggs at 1-800-379-5017

Offers and Certificates

Commit to doing everything you can to slow down the aging process and age-proof your memory. Maintain the momentum from this book through the Taylor-on-the-Brain Bulletin—SynapSez®. It is designed for you!

This free quarterly bulletin provides cutting-edge brain-function information and brain aerobic exercises to help you continue to improve your intelligent memory and challenge your neurons.

In addition, SynapSez® provides you with:

- Advance notice of new products
- Promotional discounts available to subscribers
- Seminar dates, topics, and locations
- Articles by Taylor, Briggs, and industry experts
- News items and Q&As

To start receiving SynapSez®, sign up at:

www.arlenetaylor.org

Realizations Inc and Thriving Brain will not sell, rent, or share your email or personal information with any person or company. You may unsubscribe at any time.

Books

Books by Arlene R. Taylor PhD and Sharlet M. Briggs PhD are available on Amazon.com

Seminars

Commonly requested seminars include:

- The Brain Program
- Age-Proofing Your Memory
- Age-Proofing Your Brain
- Age-Proofing Your Immune System
- The Brain and Male-Female Differences
- How the Brain Learns Best
- Upshift, Downshift, and About Shift
- The Brain and Laughter
- Build Your Business by Design

For other seminars and calendar of events go to:

www.arlenetaylor.org
www.ThrivingBrain.com/events

Ask about California C. E. credit that is available for all seminars and DVD's of 50 minutes or longer:

- RN's (CA BRN Provider #08580, Board of Registered Nurses)
- MFT's/LCSW's (CA BBS Provider #PCE37, Board of Behavioral Science)

For a list of available DVD's go to:

www.ThrivingBrain.com/products
www.arlenetaylor.org

Products also available on www.amazon.com

BTSA

The authors believe that retaining intelligent memory involves maximizing your brain's innate energy advantage. There is no greater commitment you can make to jump-start your personal and professional success than to take advantage of the BTSA (Benziger Thinking Styles Assessment).

The knowledge you can gain through this thinking-styles assessment offers you the option to use your brain energy more effectively and maximize your potential.

To discover more about this dynamic brain-function assessment, go to:

www.arlenetaylor.org/btsa

Certificates

Certificate
Two for 10% Off

DVDs

Call 1-800-379-5017
Give coupon #APYM-202

May not be combined with other promotions

Certificate
Two for 10% Off

Books

Call 1-800-379-5017
Coupon #APYM-203

May not be combined with other promotions

Certificate
10% Off

The Brain Program

Call 1-800-379-5017
Coupon #APYM-104

May not be combined with other promotions

Certificate
10% Off

Build Your Business By Design

Call 1-800-379-5017
Coupon #APYM-105

May not be combined with other promotions